Bible Study Guide

Tempted and Tried

Good Questions Have
Small Groups Talking

By Josh Hunt

Contents

Tempted and Tried Lesson #1
Slaughterhouse Drive
Good Questions Have Groups Talking
www.joshhunt.com

Slaughterhouse Drive

OPEN
What is your name and three things you are grateful for this week.

DIG

1. **Proverbs 7.6 – 21. What do we learn about dealing with temptation from this verse?**

   A fourth warning against immorality consumes the entire chapter. The victim in this case is a young man (v. 7) who is naive and untaught in moral discipline. He is at the wrong place at the wrong time (vv. 8, 9). The description of the harlot is vivid: she has the attire of a harlot (v. 10) which gives her intentions away; her character is loud and stubborn (v. 11); and her movements are all about town (v. 12). She uses shock treatment (v. 13); tells him that the time is ideal, a religious holiday (v. 14); and the place is ideal, a luxurious bedroom (vv. 16, 17). Finally, the goodman (husband) is not at home (v. 19) so there is nothing to fear. The one who so yields is as an ox goeth to the slaughter (v. 22). Since the father realizes that his sons could yield to the same temptation, he admonishes them to protect their heart, or mind (v. 25), before the time of temptation occurs. The destiny of those who commit such a sin is death (v. 27), or else a missing out on the real joy of married love. The real intimacy and pleasure that God intended in the marital act is forfeited in the adulterous relationship. — *King James Version Study Bible*., electronic ed. (Nashville: Thomas Nelson, 1997), Pr 7:1.

2. Is temptation a sin?

You get the impression that this young man is either terribly dumb or very proud, convinced that he can play with sin and get away with it. But he's only tempting himself and heading for trouble. To begin with, he's out at night ("walking in darkness"—see 2:13; John 3:19–21; 1 John 1:5–7), and he's deliberately walking near the place of temptation and danger. He didn't heed the wise counsel of the Lord, "Remove your way far from her, and do not go near the door of her house" (5:8, NKJV). God's Word wasn't controlling his feet (3:26; 4:27).

During more than forty years of ministry, I've listened to many sad stories from people who have indulged in sexual sin and suffered greatly; in almost every instance, the people deliberately put themselves into the place of temptation and danger. Unlike Job, they didn't make "a covenant with [their] eyes not to look lustfully at a girl" (Job 31:1, NIV), nor did they follow the example of Joseph and flee from temptation (Gen. 39:7ff; 2 Tim. 2:22). We can't help being tempted, but we can certainly help tempting ourselves. — Warren W. Wiersbe, *Be Skillful, "Be" Commentary Series* (Wheaton, IL: Victor Books, 1996), 55.

3. Verse 7. What does Proverbs mean when it speaks of the simple?

The young man who gives in to the immoral woman is described as simple, a term that pegs him as naive, inexperienced, and devoid of understanding (see 1:4; 9:3). He has no idea how foolish he is. He thinks he makes his way to the woman, but she in fact seduces him. — *The NKJV Study Bible* (Nashville, TN: Thomas Nelson, 2007), Proverbs 7:6–10.

4. When does temptation turn into sin? Does it do so all at once, or is it a gradual thing?

Oh, the fatal mistake of crossing the street! We are sadly mistaken if we think that we fall into temptation all at once. No, most the time it begins small and subtle. It's not the first look that trips us up; it's the lingering look that becomes the longing look. Then there is an action that takes us dangerously near. Before we know it, just like the foolish man described in the proverb, we are become trapped and snared. Whether it's the chocolate cake on the counter or the R-rated movies on your TV, or the bottle of alcohol in a cupboard, it only takes one moment of weakness for us to "cross the street." It's like a magnet; the closer we get, the harder it is to resist.

What's God's advice? "Flee . . . youthful lusts" (2 Timothy 2:22, NKJV). Shake the magnetic pull by turning around and walking away. — Debbi Bryson, *The One Year Wisdom for Women Devotional: 365 Devotions through the Proverbs* (Carol Stream, IL: Tyndale, 2013).

5. Verse 14. Who is this woman? Is she what we would think of as a church-going woman?

You can almost hear the cry of Solomon as one who has experienced these things, shouting, "Run! Resist!" The irony is that here is a woman who has spent time in fellowship, paying her vows, keeping the commandments of the Lord. And yet she seeks to ensnare this man. This happens not infrequently. People can leave a time of worship and study and somehow feel that, because they're right with the Lord, they can compromise their standards. For example, we can share things we learn in Bible study with someone from the opposite sex, but unknowingly and sometimes imperceptibly, we find ourselves getting involved in inappropriate ways. — Jon Courson, *Jon Courson's Application Commentary: Volume Two: Psalms-Malachi* (Nashville, TN: Thomas Nelson, 2006), 195.

6. What do we learn about temptation from this? What is the application?

What's the solution? The first step is awareness. We must be aware that, just because we've been in church, we're not insulated from being susceptible to this type of sin. In fact, it can make you even more vulnerable in certain ways.

Second, I believe it is expressly for protection for this kind of sin that Paul says if a woman has a question concerning something that is said in church, she's to ask her husband (1 Corinthians 14:35). It's always best for women to ask their husbands concerning spiritual matters. If you're not married, ask an older sister. If your husband isn't a Christian, ask him anyway. I know men who are part of the fellowship right now because their wives asked them spiritual questions and they themselves were driven to study the Word and to ask other brothers. And in so doing, they were saved in the process.

Jesus said that wherever a man's treasure is, there will his heart be also (Luke 12:34). If a woman pours out her treasure to a brother, suddenly, inevitably, treasure is transferred. Instead of going home and pouring out her heart to her husband, she poured it out to this individual and in so doing, planted the seeds of a potential for a relationship that will lead to problems and difficulty.

The Holy Spirit will show you when you're crossing a line. Be oh, so sensitive to His leading. It may seem initially preposterous and impossible that you are courting problems through a seemingly simple friendship. But many have been wounded. Many strong men have fallen. And not one of us is immune. That's why Solomon spends so much time saying, "Be careful."

Is there someone in your life who takes a more important role than he or she should, anyone who is dependent upon you, or upon whom you're dependent? Is there anyone whose path crosses yours more than necessary? Is there anyone interested in you that shouldn't be? Run for your life. Put up a barrier. Do what it takes. If the Holy Spirit is leading, listen to His leading. When the Lord wants to change my mind or change my heart or change my ways, I initially want to change the subject. But it is the wise man, the wise woman who listens and determines to do the wise thing. — Jon Courson, *Jon Courson's Application Commentary: Volume Two: Psalms-Malachi* (Nashville, TN: Thomas Nelson, 2006), 195.

7. How is this simple man like an ox going to the slaughter?

That is the price one pays for adultery and immorality. As a pastor, I have come face to face with the wounds of immorality many, many times. I see it in airports as I travel— crying children being swapped between divorced parents as they are shuttled between two different "homes." I see it in the pain and anguish of betrayal, the humiliation of having been used and abused, and the shadows of broken dreams which are still there every morning. The tragic results of immorality afflict the church in almost the same proportions as they do the world. Perhaps the pictures of the effects of immorality in Proverbs will help to awaken our senses to the dangers that lie in wait. — David Jeremiah, *Powerful Principles from Proverbs: Study Guide* (Nashville, TN: Thomas Nelson Publishers, 2002), 35.

8. James 5.1 – 5. Who is James addressing in this passage?

James' attack in the opening paragraph of chapter 5 can only be described as seething. It is so fierce that Upton Sinclair, the novelist and social reformer, once read a paraphrase of this section to a group of ministers after attributing it to Emma Goldman, an anarchist agitator. The ministers were so enraged they declared she ought to be deported! So we must take heed as we preach and teach this passage lest we be likewise disposed of! But we must also take heed, for this is God's Word and we will all answer to him who will judge our souls for eternity.

Actually James' invective is aimed at his wealthy, nonbelieving countrymen who were exploiting the poor, many of whom were in the church. Specifically, James' targets were wealthy farmers who owned large tracts of land and were squeezing everyone and everything for profit. But though these persons were the calloused unbelieving rich, the message is also meant to benefit the church. James understood that the natural human tendency to envy the rich, if sustained, would lead many Christians astray. Thus, this scathing warning to the ungodly rich is also meant to steel his people against such folly. In addition, James' terrifying description of the judgment awaiting these rich countrymen is meant to ensure the exploited poor that justice is coming and they ought to bear their indignities with patience.

This is a timely message for us as we all live under the lure of "The Lifestyles of the Rich and Famous"—the seductive delusion that "you are what you buy." May the Holy Spirit help us to step inside James' smoldering human spirit, hear the hammer blows as he pounds the arrogant rich, and allow those blows to shape our lives as well. — R. Kent Hughes, *James: Faith That Works, Preaching the Word* (Wheaton, IL: Crossway Books, 1991), 211–212.

9. Is it bad to be rich?

Echoing the voice of many prophets, James tells the rich to "weep and wail" (NIV) or "weep and howl" (ESV). The judgment of God is coming and will bring them misery. On the one hand, James does not condemn everyone who is rich. Chapter 1 shows that among his readers were some rich believers (James 1:10). Further, many heroes of the faith were wealthy: Abraham, Joseph, Job, David, and Solomon in the Old Testament; Joseph of Arimathea and Zacchaeus in the New. Riches are not evil in themselves. On the other hand, Jesus says, "It is easier for a camel to go through the eye of a needle than for a rich man to enter the kingdom of God" (Matt. 19:24). The desire for wealth is often insatiable. "Whoever loves money never has money enough; whoever loves wealth is never satisfied with his income" (Eccl. 5:10). — Daniel M. Doriani, *James*, ed. Richard D. Phillips, Philip Graham Ryken, and Daniel M. Doriani, Reformed Expository Commentary (Phillipsburg, NJ: P&R Publishing, 2007), 167.

10. What was the temptation of this crowd?

James suggests it was rich people's hoarding and self-indulgence that assured their bleak future under God's coming judgment. Contrary to human logic, hoarding doesn't avoid future problems; it causes them! — Randy Alcorn, *Managing God's Money: A Biblical Guide* (Carol Stream, IL: Tyndale, 2011).

11. How are they like fattened cows?

Let that soak in. Like a cow who is gorging himself on food moments before he goes to the slaughter. This is the picture of people who gorge themselves on luxury and self-indulgence, he says, enjoying it all when the reality is in an instant you're going to be slaughtered. What a picture. If this is not a stern enough warning against the luxury self-indulgent inherent in our culture's ideals and values. — David Platt, "Faith Lasts," *in David Platt Sermon Archive* (Birmingham, AL: David Platt, 2009), 2276.

12. What do we learn about temptation from this passage? What is the application?

Jesus' brother James knew the language of the slaughterhouse. A Christian bishop in Jerusalem soon after the dawn of the church, James warned the rich and contented of his day that living in "luxury and in self-indulgence" couldn't rescue them. "You have fattened your hearts in a day of slaughter," he thundered (James 5:5). James knew this partly from personal experience. He hadn't always been a holy man. As a kid he'd probably laughed at his brother—just like the rest of his kin and neighbors—as a delusional egotist at best, a demon-possessed cultist at worst. But he came to see his brother as something very different—as the express image of God and as the rightful ruler of the universe.

James knew what it was like to live in an illusion, and what it was like to wake from it. He warned the little Christian assemblies dotting the landscape in the generation after Jesus' resurrection that they would need a supernatural kind of spiritual wisdom in order to see where temptation lurks and to recognize the path it takes (James 1:5). The awful truth is that we are fallen creatures, and as such are in constant danger of being "lured" (James 1:14). Temptation—for the entire human race, for the people of Israel, and for each of us personally—starts with a question of identity, moves to a confusion of the desires, and ultimately heads to a contest of futures. In short, there's a reason you want what you don't want to want. Temptation is embryonic, personality specific, and purpose directed.

Something is afoot out there that's deeper and older and scarier than we can contemplate. The Christian Scriptures propose an answer to the question, What's wrong with me? Before you wrestle with the temptation in your own life, you'll need to see the horror of what it really is, as well as the glory of how Jesus triumphs over it. Jesus walked through the cycle of temptation for us, and does so with us. Like "a lamb that is led to the slaughter" (Isa. 53:7), he walked out into the wilderness and onto the stairway to hell. — Russell D. Moore, *Tempted and Tried: Temptation and the Triumph of Christ* (Wheaton, IL: Crossway, 2011).

13. Matthew 4:1. Context. Note the word, "then." What does that refer to?

"Then Jesus was led up by the Spirit into the wilderness to be tempted by the devil," the Gospel accounts tell us (Matt. 4:1). The fourth-century Christian leader John Chrysostom was right to note that the word "then" is crucially significant here. It is only "then" that Jesus went into the desert—that is, after his identity was publicly marked out by his Father. In order to understand the temptations of Jesus, we have to understand that Jesus' hair was still wet when he stepped out into the desert.

The Scriptures tell us that Jesus started his public ministry by finding his cousin, a prophet named John who was baptizing out in the wilderness, and requesting baptism. That probably sounds fairly predictable and noncontroversial, if you think of baptism as simply a religious ritual. But it's much more than that. If you had watched from the hillside, you might have noticed a long awkward conversation as the prophet and his cousin seemed to be discussing something—no, debating something. The baptizer was waving his hands, shrugging his shoulders, but then he stopped and walked with his cousin out into the river. What you would have seen is what the Gospels record as John reluctantly doing what Jesus asked him to do—to baptize him.

John's dismayed confusion is entirely appropriate. This baptism is, after all, a sign of God's judgment. That's why it is about repentance. Those "vipers" coming down to the river have been "warned" of the "wrath to come" (Matt. 3:7). By going through the water, they're acknowledging that they deserve God's winnowing fire at the Day of Judgment. As they are cleansed beneath the river, they are calling out with "an appeal to God for a good conscience" (1 Pet. 3:21), that they might be saved when the flood of his anger falls. To hear Jesus' request to be baptized would have felt to John the way it would feel to you to hear your spouse announce an interest in being listed on a registry of child molesters. Yet it was necessary, Jesus told him, "to fulfill all righteousness" (Matt. 3:15). Jesus wasn't disputing John's assessment of his identity; he was confirming it. He was indeed the Lamb of God who would take away the sins of the world by bearing them on himself. Jesus was saying to John, in effect, "You can't understand who I am without understanding who my God is, that's true; but you also can't understand who I am without understanding who my people are."

As you observed the scene, you would have noticed a tumult run through the crowd as the cousins came up out of the water. A strange presence would have shot down from somewhere above you—what you would later be told was the Holy Spirit coming down, like a dove, on this Jesus (Matt. 3:16). Even more astounding, there would be a thunderous voice coming from the skies announcing, "This is my beloved Son, with whom I am well pleased" (Matt. 3:17).

It is impossible to understand the temptations without seeing the baptism. Water is wild. Your body is made mostly of it, and you need it to live, but it can drown you. It can sweep away your life in a flood. In the early moments of creation, we're told that the "formless and void" wild earth was covered with water, "and the Spirit of God was moving over the surface of the waters" (Gen. 1:2 NASB). The image the Bible most often uses for unpredictable danger is that of the sea, a sea the Scripture promises will give up its dead and will be no more in the coming kingdom (Rev. 21:1).

Here, in the water, Jesus identified himself with us, and God identified himself with Jesus. In every one of the temptations, Satan attempted to counteract God's voice at this point: "If you are the son of God, then . . ." This is the equivalent of the Edenic "Has God really said?" The baptism was an inauguration of Jesus' kingship, and it was a declaration of war. — Russell D. Moore, *Tempted and Tried: Temptation and the Triumph of Christ* (Wheaton, IL: Crossway, 2011).

14. What does "then" teach us about temptation?

It is often true that after the blessings come the battles. On the heels of His baptism, the Spirit led Jesus into the wilderness, where He would encounter the enemy. — Jon Courson, *Jon Courson's Application Commentary* (Nashville, TN: Thomas Nelson, 2003), 20.

15. We use the word "temptation" in church a lot. What exactly does it mean?

The chapter begins by saying, "Then Jesus was led by the Spirit into the desert to be tempted by the devil" (Matt. 4:1). Since the initiative in this account is with God—the verse says, "Jesus was led by the Spirit into the desert to be tempted"—the necessary starting place for this study must be the nature of the "temptation." In English the word tempt has come to mean almost without exception "tempt to do evil." But the word for tempt in Hebrew and Greek means "to test or prove." This can include a tempting to do evil, but it often means only a "testing to prove the value or good quality of," just as a person might test gold by submersing it in acid. If the gold is pure, nothing happens. If it is not, the impurity is burned off.

It was in this sense that Abraham was "tested" by God when he was called to sacrifice his son Isaac, and Job was tested by the things that happened to him. When the Spirit led Jesus into the desert to be tempted by Satan, the act was a test designed to show that Jesus really was God's Son and that he would follow the path God had laid out for him. — James Montgomery Boice, *The Gospel of Matthew* (Grand Rapids, MI: Baker Books, 2001), 54.

16. Does God test (or tempt) us?

This time of testing showed that Jesus really was the Son of God, able to overcome the devil and his temptations. A person has not shown true obedience if he or she has never had an opportunity to disobey. We read in Deuteronomy 8:2–3 that God led Israel into the desert to humble and test them. God wanted to see whether or not his people would really obey him. You too will be tested. Because you know that testing will come, you should be alert and ready for it. Remember, your convictions are only real if they hold up under pressure! — Bruce B. Barton, *Matthew*, Life Application Bible Commentary (Wheaton, IL: Tyndale House Publishers, 1996), 56.

17. What was God's purpose in this temptation?

The word "then" indicates an important connection of the end of chapter 3 and the beginning of chapter 4. The same Holy Spirit that sent Jesus to be baptized, then sent Jesus into the wilderness. The temptation was a divine necessity to prove Jesus' messianic purpose. Led up by the Spirit, Jesus took the offensive against the enemy, Satan, by going into the lonely and desolate wilderness to face temptation. In the Old Testament, the "wilderness" (or "desert") was a desolate and dangerous place where wild animals lived (see, for example, Isaiah 13:20–22; 34:8–15). — Bruce B. Barton, *Matthew*, Life

Application Bible Commentary (Wheaton, IL: Tyndale House Publishers, 1996), 54–55.

18. What was Satan's purpose in the temptation?

But that is only from God's point of view! It was God's purpose. From the point of view of the devil and his purpose, the temptation was evil, for it was an attempt to get Jesus to question God's word, misuse God's promises in Scripture, and try to win the world for himself by linking up with Satan rather than by going to the cross. — James Montgomery Boice, *The Gospel of Matthew* (Grand Rapids, MI: Baker Books, 2001), 54.

19. What does the Bible teach about the Devil? Who is he? Where did he come from? What is his goal?

"Devil" in Greek means "accuser"; in Hebrew, the word "Satan" means the same (4:10). The devil tempted Eve in the Garden of Eden, and here he tempted Jesus in the wilderness. Satan is a fallen archangel. He is a real, created being, not symbolic, and is constantly fighting against those who follow and obey God. The verb "to be tempted" describes continuous action because Jesus was tempted constantly during the forty days. The word "tempted" means "to put to the test to see what good or evil, strengths or weaknesses, exist in a person." The Spirit compelled Jesus into the wilderness where God put Jesus to the test—not to see if Jesus was ready, but to show that he was ready for his mission. Satan, however, had other plans; he hoped to thwart Jesus' mission by tempting Jesus to do evil. Satan tried to get Jesus to declare his kingship prematurely. Satan tried to get Jesus to take his messianic power into his own hands and to forsake his Father's will. If Jesus had given in, his mission on earth—to die for our sins and give us the opportunity to have eternal life—would have been lost. For more on Satan, see 1 Chronicles 21:1; Job 1–2; Zechariah 3:1–2; Luke 10:18; Revelation 20. — Bruce B. Barton, *Matthew*, Life Application Bible Commentary (Wheaton, IL: Tyndale House Publishers, 1996), 54–55.

20. **We will be getting more into this in weeks to come, but let's look at an overview of this temptation story. What do we learn about our own temptation from this story?**

How can we resist temptation? Consider what Jesus did—He quoted scripture. (See Matthew 4:1–11 and Luke 4:1–13.) Satan tried to get Jesus to yield to the lust of the flesh by performing a self-serving miracle to satisfy His hunger. "It is written..." Jesus answered. Satan also appealed to the lust of the eyes by offering Him all the kingdoms of the world to possess early (thus bypassing crucifixion). Again Jesus said, "It is written..." The pride of life was a third temptation Jesus faced. Satan even quoted scripture, twisting it to entice Jesus to misuse His power in order to promote Himself. For the third time, Jesus quoted from Deuteronomy and said, "Away with you, Satan!" (Matthew 4:10 NKJV).

We experience temptations in these same areas—desire to do things we shouldn't (passions), desire to have (possessions), and desire to be more important (pride). Do we have scriptures as our defense? Find verses to fight your greatest areas of weakness. Memorize them and draw them like a sword when tempted by the world, the flesh, and the devil. — Renae Brumbaugh et al., *One-a Daily Devotional: One Way, One Truth, One Life* (Uhrichsville, OH: Barbour, 2015).

21. **How can we support one another in prayer this week?**

Envision yourself as a small group leader with people who don't know how to pray or are intimidated by prayer. You are not going to start out with deep, joy-filled times of prayer. It can be extremely awkward at first, but with practice you will find prayer can be the part of the small group that people look forward to the most. Here are some suggestions related to what you can pray for and how you can initiate group prayer:

Deciding what to pray for.

To start with, you could occupy your time praying for each member of the group, asking God to help you grow in Christ. Most groups don't do this enough because it feels uncomfortable at first, but you should seek to strengthen each other by name in prayer. Then, you could pray for any of the following:

- personal needs shared in the group

- family and friends of group members

- the needs of your church or fellowship group

- sick, shut-in, suffering and/or bereaved people that group members know

- non-Christian friends, family and/or neighbors

- missions and missionaries

- and don't forget worship!

You might also go back through the sections on worship, confession and petition and make your own list of possible prayer items.

As you pray for these and other requests, you may want to keep a "prayer notebook" so that you can record answered prayers and further enhance group worship. — Jeffrey Arnold and Stephanie Black, *The Big Book on Small Groups* (Downers Grove, IL: InterVarsity Press, 1992).

Tempted and Tried Lesson #2
Starving to Death
Good Questions Have Groups Talking
www.joshhunt.com

Starving to Death

OPEN

What is your name and when was the last time you were really, really hungry.

DIG

1. **Matthew 4.1 – 11. Overview. What do we learn about dealing with temptation from Jesus' example of dealing with temptation?**

    We're often told that Jesus quoted Scripture to the devil and thereby defeated him. But it wasn't quite that easy. There were other factors involved in gaining victory. Through reading the story of the Temptation in Matthew 4, we notice that Jesus also relied on the Holy Spirit, who was leading Him at every point (verse 1). Christ was maintaining the spiritual discipline of fasting, and we can assume He was in the middle of a season of prayer (verse 2). Our Lord was also determined to say, "No! No! No!" to Satan's three enticements. Verse 11 tells us that Jesus outlasted the temptation and Satan limped away in defeat after being worn out by our Lord's unflinching righteousness. Within that context, Jesus quoted Scripture three times to Satan and thereby won the victory.

To win against sin, we need the Holy Spirit's power, the practice of regular spiritual disciplines, a determination to live righteously, tenacity, and a handful of crucial Scriptures to quote in times of temptation.

With our spiritual tools ready, we, too, can resist the devil, and he will flee from us. — David Jeremiah, *Discovering God: 365 Daily Devotions* (Carol Stream, IL: Tyndale, 2015).

2. How would you turn this passage into a prayer?

Lord God, in the days of His flesh, when Jesus had offered up prayers and supplications, with vehement cries and tears to You who were able to save Him from death, and was heard because of His godly fear, though He was a Son, yet He learned obedience by the things which He suffered. And having been perfected, He became the author of eternal salvation to all who obey Him. I do not have a High Priest who cannot sympathize with my weaknesses, but was in all points tempted as I am, yet without sin.

No temptation has overtaken me except such as is common to man; but You, Lord God, are faithful, who will not allow me to be tempted beyond what I am able, but with the temptation will also make the way of escape, that I may be able to bear it. Your grace is sufficient for me, for Your strength is made perfect in weakness. — David Jeremiah, *Life-Changing Moments With God* (Nashville, TN: Thomas Nelson Publishers, 2007), 206.

3. Let's start with a doctrinal question. A key point of Christian doctrine has to do with the identity or nature of Christ. He was 100% God and 100% man. How does this passage teach us the humanity of Christ?

When Jesus did not drink, he got thirsty. When he ate nothing for forty days, he grew hungry. He knew he could use his powers selfishly, to turn those stones to bread, but he refused. Both the temptation and the response fit the fabric of Jesus' life, a real human life. As a man, Jesus was susceptible to temptation. — Daniel M. Doriani, *Matthew*

& 2, ed. Richard D. Phillips, Philip Graham Ryken, and Daniel M. Doriani, vol. 1, Reformed Expository Commentary (Phillipsburg, NJ: P&R Publishing, 2008), 73.

4. Why is it important that we embrace the doctrine of the humanity of Christ? What would change if we did not believe in the humanity of Christ?

The doctrine of the humanity of Jesus is vital to the Christian faith. If Jesus had not become man, there would be no forgiveness of sin and, consequently, no possibility of a relationship with God. But there is much more. The fact that Jesus became fully human

- changes how I pray (I know that He can relate to me and understand me),

- helps me when I face temptation (I know that He dealt with it too),

- consoles me when I am down, (I know He faced great disappointments), and

- strengthens me when I feel weak (I know He experienced sickness and the limitations of bodily existence).

Just as understanding and believing the deity of Christ is indispensable to our faith, so also is appreciating His humanity. — *Discipleship Journal, Issue 148* (July/August 2005) (NavPress, 2005).

5. Jesus memorized Scripture and used it to defeat the Devil. Do you think Scripture memory is important?

Most Christians don't like to hear the "Bible memory" message, but I'm going to summarize here because it is so important in defeating temptation. How did Jesus defeat Satan in the wilderness? By quoting the Word of God. And we can do the same (Matthew 4:1–11). If Jesus relied on Bible memory, do you think it might be good for us as well? One of the best verses I know to memorize as a great checklist for

Internet use is Philippians 4:8: "Finally, brethren, whatever things are true . . . noble . . . just . . . pure . . . lovely . . . of good report, if there is any virtue and if there is anything praiseworthy—meditate on these things." If you can find a web site that meets those criteria, then stay there all day. If it doesn't, then you'd better move on in a hurry.

When we hide God's Word in our hearts the Holy Spirit can bring it immediately to mind when we are tempted (Psalm 119:9, 11). To use computer terminology, some Christians' hard drives are completely empty—there is nothing stored there for the Holy Spirit to use to help them resist sin. So start downloading the Word today. — David Jeremiah, *Family Factor: Study Guide* (Nashville, TN: Thomas Nelson Publishers, 2003), 96.

6. Just for fun, let's see how many verses we can quote. Who will go first?

In his book *The Lost Art of Disciple Making*, LeRoy Eims describes his personal battle with anger. It was not until he made a covenant with God, which included memorizing and meditating on Colossians 3:8 ("You yourselves are to put off all these: anger, wrath . . ."), that anger loosened its grip on his emotions. He reviewed the verse daily and asked the Lord to bring it to mind whenever he was tempted to lose his temper. The Word of God became a sword with which he was able to win his spiritual battle.

Jesus used Scripture in a similar way. When He was tempted for forty days and nights in the wilderness by Satan, Jesus rebuffed every temptation by quoting an appropriate verse from Deuteronomy (Matthew 4:1-11). If you are in a spiritual battle, your sword is to be the Word of God —the sword of the Spirit (Ephesians 6:17). If there is a persistent spiritual battle you fight, memorize a portion of God's living and active Word to gain the victory. — David Jeremiah, *Discovering God: 365 Daily Devotions* (Carol Stream, IL: Tyndale, 2015).

7. I'd like to challenge you to memorize two verses a week until you have 100 verses. Who will join me in this challenge?

15 benefits of filling your mind with God's word by Francis Cosgrove

1. INCREASING OUR FAITH

Scripture memory increases our faith and trust in God. We begin to look at life more and more from his point of view. Paul wrote, "Your attitude should be the same as that of Christ Jesus" (Philippians 2:5). The memorized word of God helps us grasp this attitude of Christ as we walk through life, and builds our faith in God's guidance and love for us.

Christian worker Bob Foster called Scripture memory "the daily habit of supplying the subconscious with God's material to chew upon." He wrote,

> There is a vast difference between "I have a verse" and "It has me." The one can be the parrot-like repetition of words . . . the latter is the transforming by the renewing of your mind.

2. VICTORY OVER SIN

Just as the psalmist wrote, Scripture memory helps us have victory over sin: "I have hidden your word in my heart that I might not sin against you" (Psalm 119:11).

3. INNER CLEANSING

Scripture memory has a cleansing effect. To get rid of unclean thoughts which can lead to unclean words and actions, we can substitute clean thoughts by concentrating on the words of God that we have memorized. Instead of suppressing evil thoughts, we replace them.

4. KNOWING BIBLE DOCTRINE

Scripture memory can increase our awareness of biblical doctrines, providing a practical foundation for the way we are to live.

5. GUIDANCE

God instructs us in the way we should go as he speaks to us through the Scriptures we know by heart. "Your statutes are my delight; they are my counselors" (Psalm 119:24).

6. PRAYER

Jesus said, "If you remain in me and my words remain in you, ask whatever you wish, and it will be given you" (John 15:7). Our prayer life is enhanced as we pray Scripture back to God.

7. BIBLE STUDY

Scripture memory helps us in our study of the Bible. We know more cross-references, and we can more easily tie various parts of Scripture together to increase our understanding.

8. FINDING PASSAGES

By memorizing key verses, we can locate specific passages on a particular teaching. Knowing Matthew 6:33, for example— "But seek first his kingdom and his righteousness, and all these things will be given to you as well"—helps us remember that Jesus's teaching about placing God's concerns above our own physical needs is found in Matthew 6.

9. MEDITATION

Scripture memory allows us to meditate at any time on God's word. We'll always have something scriptural to think about, even when it isn't possible to open up a Bible. "Oh, how I love your law! I meditate on it all day long" (Psalm 119:97).

10. EXPERIENCING THE HOLY SPIRIT

The Holy Spirit uses the Scriptures we have memorized to strengthen us and to help us experience the power of his presence.

11. WORSHIP

Scripture memory helps us worship God. In our personal, joyful worship of him at any time of day we can praise God with Scripture. "Seven times a day I praise you for your righteous laws" (Psalm 119:164).

12. NOT WASTING TIME

Scripture memory helps us make good use of what might otherwise be wasted time, such as waiting in a long line at the grocery store or driving to work. We may even find that occupying our mind with God's word keeps us from becoming impatient or angry.

13. COUNSELING

Scripture memory helps us in counseling others. We will be able to say what the prophet Isaiah said: "The Sovereign Lord has given me an instructed tongue, to know the word that sustains the weary" (Isaiah 50:4). The Holy Spirit will bring to our mind verses that suit the particular need of the person we are talking with.

14. WITNESSING

Scripture memory enables us to witness effectively. By knowing verses that present the plan of salvation we are equipped for evangelism at any time, just as the apostle Peter quoted the Old Testament words of Joel and David as he spoke to the crowd that assembled on the day of Pentecost (Acts 2). We can also give biblical answers to people who ask us about our faith. We may not have a Bible with us in a spur-of-the-moment situation, but we are never without the Scripture portions we have memorized.

15. TEACHING

Anyone who teaches God's word publicly should be able to quote Scripture to make his points and to answer questions from his listeners. — From *Essentials of Discipleship* (NavPress, 1980). / Discipleship Journal, Issue 9 (May/June 1982) (NavPress, 1982).

8. How does Scripture memory aid our prayer life?

The Word of God is a great help in prayer. If it is lodged and written in our hearts, it will form an outflowing current of prayer, full and irresistible. Promises, stored in the heart, are to be the fuel from which prayer receives life and warmth. Just as coal, which has been stored in the earth, ministers to our comfort on stormy days and wintry nights, the Word of God stored in our hearts is the food by which prayer is nourished and made strong. Prayer, like man, cannot live by bread alone, "but by every word that proceedeth out of the mouth of God" (Matthew 4:4 KJV).

Unless the vital forces of prayer are supplied by God's Word, prayer, though earnest, even vociferous in its urgency, is, in reality, flabby and void. —E. M. BOUNDS / Thomas Nelson, *A Daybook of Prayer: Meditations, Scriptures and Prayers to Draw near to the Heart of God* (Nashville: Thomas Nelson, 2006).

9. Do a search in the app store for Scripture memory apps. Download one or two.

My favorite is Scripture Typer.

10. Verse 3. What is the essence of this first temptation? To what temptation that we might have would you compare it?

Most of the commentators on Matthew understand these words to be an admission that Jesus really was God's Son (meaning, "Since you are the Son of God ...") and thus merely a temptation to abuse his status by a misuse of his divine power. This would have been a genuine temptation, of course; it would have been a temptation to doubt God's willingness or ability to care for Jesus as a Son and perhaps also to misuse his divine power to avoid the sufferings inherent in his having assumed human nature. Yet I think R. C. Sproul is right when he suggests that the emphasis is on the word if ("If you are the Son of God ..."). In this case, the temptation's focus lies in questioning God's earlier statement.

Back in Eden, to which this account is certainly connected, Adam and Eve were tempted to doubt the word of God. God had told them that they would die if they ate from the fruit of the forbidden tree, but Satan countered, "You will not surely die" (Gen. 3:4). Here, in a similar manner, Satan suggests that Jesus may not actually be God's Son, or, if he is, he should settle any doubts on the matter once and for all by a miracle. Thus, it was a temptation to question the express word of God hidden under what seemed to be a concern for Jesus' physical hunger. — James Montgomery Boice, *The Gospel of Matthew* (Grand Rapids, MI: Baker Books, 2001), 56.

11. Compare this temptation with Genesis 3.1. What do they have in common? What do we learn about temptation from this?

The devil's first approach to Jesus had also been his first approach to Eve to cast doubt on God's Word. He asked Eve, "Indeed, has God said, 'You shall not eat from any tree of the garden'?" (Gen. 3:1), causing her to question God's command. His first word to Jesus was, If you are the Son of God-the Greek conditional phrase assumes that Jesus is indeed the divine Son whom the Father had just proclaimed Him to be at His baptism (3:17). Before he gave the direct temptation, Satan gave this one simply to set up the rest. Satan was hoping to persuade Jesus to demonstrate His power to verify that it was real. That would mean violating God's plan that He set that power aside in humiliation and use it only when the Father willed. Satan wanted Jesus to disobey God. Affirming His deity and rights as the Son of God would have been to act independently of God. — John

F. MacArthur Jr., *Matthew, MacArthur New Testament Commentary* (Chicago: Moody Press, 1985), 90.

12. What exactly does it mean, "Man does not live by bread alone"?

Jesus had no trouble answering Satan. He did it by quoting a verse from Deuteronomy: "It is written: 'Man does not live on bread alone, but on every word that comes from the mouth of God' " (Matt. 4:4; see Deut. 8:3). If the temptation were only to misuse his supernatural power, Jesus' reply would not be directly to the point. But if the temptation were to doubt the word of God by testing it, Jesus' answer would mean, "It does not really matter much whether I have physical bread to eat, since God will preserve my life as long as he wants so I can do what he wants. I trust him in that. What does matter is whether I believe God's word implicitly or not. If I should doubt his word, even for a moment, all is lost." — James Montgomery Boice, *The Gospel of Matthew* (Grand Rapids, MI: Baker Books, 2001), 56.

13. Matthew 4.4. What does it mean that we are to live by every Word that comes from the mouth of God?

To make sense, to find satisfaction in this life, we need God's word. Because Jesus knew this, he could look beyond his hunger, his desire for bread. He could refuse to take the bread that was good, but not his at this time, by the Father's will. Thus he passed the test that Israel failed. He did not live for physical satisfaction; he was the one true Israelite. — Daniel M. Doriani, *Matthew* & 2, ed. Richard D. Phillips, Philip Graham Ryken, and Daniel M. Doriani, vol. 1, Reformed Expository Commentary (Phillipsburg, NJ: P&R Publishing, 2008), 79.

14. We always want to read the Bible for _____ [application]. We want to be _____ [doers] of the Word and not _____ [hearers only]. What is the application of this verse that says, "man shall not live by bread alone..."?

Trust God's Word. Don't trust your emotions. Don't trust your opinions. Don't even trust your friends....

Jesus told Satan, "Man shall not live on bread alone, but on every word that proceeds out of the mouth of God." The verb proceeds is literally "pouring out." Its tense suggests that God is constantly and aggressively communicating with the world through his Word. God is speaking still! — Max Lucado, *Everyday Blessings: Inspirational Thoughts from the Published Works of Max Lucado.* (Nashville, TN: Thomas Nelson, Inc., 2004).

15. Is Jesus talking just about bread, or is there application other things?

I write these lines during a study leave at the beachfront home of a friend. Besides the beach, there are golf, tennis, sailing, fishing and more. Yet many of the people on our street are profoundly unhappy. The owner of the grandest home takes no pleasure in it, another person is feuding with almost all her neighbors, another is a virtual recluse. Material prosperity cannot guarantee happiness. I do not claim that all Christians are happy; some are not. But whatever life brings, God's word can interpret it for us. Then we will not think, "I must have that," nor will we ask our possessions to supply what God alone can give. Then we can enjoy material blessings for what they are—God's creation, meant as a secondary blessing (cf. Eccl. 1, 5). — Daniel M. Doriani, *Matthew* & 2, ed. Richard D. Phillips, Philip Graham Ryken, and Daniel M. Doriani, vol. 1, Reformed Expository Commentary (Phillipsburg, NJ: P&R Publishing, 2008), 79.

16. **Psalm 63 is a great Psalm. It records David's great hunger and thirst for God—and his great satisfaction in God. David was a man after God's own heart who lived by every Word that comes from the mouth of God. What is he feeling as he pens this words?**

To be able to say "my God" by faith transformed David's wilderness experience into a worship experience. There in the desert, he was hungry and thirsty, but his deepest desires were spiritual, not physical. With his whole being, body and soul, he yearned for God's satisfying presence (v. 5; 42:1–2). Just as we have physical senses that are satisfied by God's creation, so we have spiritual senses (Heb. 5:14) that can be satisfied only by Christ. He is the bread of life (John 6), and He gives us the water of life by His Spirit (John 4:1–14; 7:37–39; Rev. 22:17). Those who hunger and thirst for spiritual food and drink shall be filled (Matt. 5:6). David could say with Jesus, "I have food to eat of which you do not know" (John 4:32, NKJV). — Warren W. Wiersbe, *Be Worshipful, 1st ed., "Be" Commentary Series* (Colorado Springs, CO: Cook Communications Ministries, 2004), 212.

17. **How is David's walk with God different from many church-goers?**

There are three types of people in any Christian gathering. There are those who are Christians in name only. They seem to be following after God and Jesus Christ and say they are, but theirs is a false following, like that of the five foolish virgins who did not truly know the Lord and were rejected by him. The second class are those who are following Jesus but are following "at a distance," like Peter at the time of Jesus' arrest. The third type are those who, as Murdoch Campbell suggests, "in storm and sunshine, cleave to him and enjoy daily communion with him." These people want God, and they want him intensely, because they know that he and he alone will satisfy the deep longing of their souls. David was a person who desired God above everything else, and Psalm 63 is a classic expression of this longing. — James Montgomery

Boice, *Psalms 42–106: An Expositional Commentary* (Grand Rapids, MI: Baker Books, 2005), 516.

18. How did David acquire this wonderful spiritual appetite? How can we develop a hunger for God?

By worshiping God at the sanctuary (v. 2; see 27:4; 84:1–2). He had erected the tent on Mt. Zion and returned the ark to its rightful place, and he had found great delight in going there and contemplating God (36:8–9; 46:4). Because he didn't belong to the tribe of Levi, David couldn't enter the sanctuary proper, but from his study of the Books of Moses, he knew the design and the assigned rituals, and he understood their deeper meaning. It is our regular worship that prepares us for the crisis experiences of life. What life does to us depends on what life finds in us, and David had in him a deep love for the Lord and a desire to please Him. Because David had seen God's power and glory in His house, he was able to see it in the wilderness as well! — Warren W. Wiersbe, *Be Worshipful, 1st ed., "Be" Commentary Series* (Colorado Springs, CO: Cook Communications Ministries, 2004), 213.

19. Summary. What do we learn about following God from this Psalm and Jesus' teaching, "Man shall not live by bread alone"?

I personally can't imagine life without bread! That's how important the Bible should be to us. — Steve Russo, *Random Thoughts: Get Real with God, Others, and Yourself* (Uhrichsville, OH: Barbour, 2011).

20. How can we support one another in prayer this week?

Tempted and Tried Lesson #3
Free Falling
Good Questions Have Groups Talking
www.joshhunt.com

Free Falling

OPEN

What is your name and, did you ever fall out of a tree, or off a ladder?

DIG

1. **Did anyone get a chance to use a Scripture memory app? What progress did you make in memorizing Scripture?**

   As you start to memorize a verse—

   • Read in your Bible the context of the verse.

   • Try to gain a clear understanding of what the verse actually means. You may want to read it in other Bible translations or paraphrases to get a better grasp of the meaning.

   • Read the verse several times thoughtfully, aloud or in a whisper. This will help you grasp the verse as a whole. Each time you read it, say the reference, then the verse, then the reference again.

   • Discuss the verse with God in prayer, and continue to seek his help for success in Scripture memory.

While you are memorizing a verse—

• Say the verse aloud as much as possible.

• Learn the reference first.

• After learning the reference, learn the first phrase of the verse. Once you have learned the reference and first phrase and have repeated them correctly several times, add more phrases one by one.

• Think about how the verse applies to you and your daily circumstances.

• Always include the reference as part of the verse as you learn and review it. Repeat the reference both before and after the verse.

After you can quote the verse correctly—

• You'll find it helpful to write out the verse. This deepens the impression in your mind.

• Review the verse immediately after learning it, and repeat it frequently in the next few days. This is crucial for fixing the verse firmly in mind, because of how quickly we tend to forget something we've recently learned.

• REVIEW! REVIEW! REVIEW! Repetition is the best way to engrave the verses on your memory.

Discipleship Journal, Issue 9 (May/June 1982) (NavPress, 1982).

2. **Matthew 4.1 – 11. Overview. What do you learn about how to deal with temptation from this passage?**

Satan is not absent from or peripheral to God's story. He is at its center. We can't understand God's narrative without understanding Satan's strategy. In fact, "the reason the Son of God appeared was to destroy the works of the devil" (1 John 3:8 ESV).

Nothing thrills Satan more than the current skepticism with which he is viewed. When people deny his existence or chalk up his works to the ills of society, he rubs his hands with glee. The more we doubt his very existence, the more he can work without hindrance.

Jesus didn't doubt the reality of the devil. The Savior strode into the badlands with one goal, to unmask Satan, and made him the first stop on his itinerary. "Then Jesus was led by the Spirit into the wilderness to be tempted by the devil" (Matthew 4:1).

Does God do the same with us? Might the Spirit of God lead us into the wilderness? If I were the devil, I'd tell you no. I would want you to think that I, on occasion, snooker heaven. That I catch God napping. That I sneak in when he isn't looking and snatch his children out of his hand. I'd leave you sleeping with one eye open.

But Scripture reveals otherwise. The next time you hear the phrase "all hell broke loose," correct the speaker. Hell does not break loose. God uses Satan's temptation to strengthen us. (If I were the devil, that would aggravate me to no end.) Times of testing are actually times of training, purification, and strength building. You can even "consider it pure joy ... whenever you face trials of many kinds, because you know that the testing of your faith produces perseverance" (James 1:2–3).

God loves you too much to leave you undeveloped and immature. "God disciplines us for our good, that we may share in his holiness. No discipline seems pleasant at the time, but painful. Later on, however, it produces a harvest of righteousness and peace for those who have been trained by it" (Hebrews 12:10–11). Expect to be tested by the devil.

And watch for his tricks. You can know what to expect. "We are not ignorant of his schemes" (2 Corinthians 2:11 NASB). — Max Lucado, *God's Story, Your Story: When His Becomes Yours* (Grand Rapids, MI: Zondervan, 2011).

3. **Why do you suppose Jesus never used any of His own words in dealing with the devil? What is the lesson for us?**

This is hard for me to comprehend. The Son of God—the One who knows all things and has the power to do all things, the One whose words we study, memorize, and meditate on—never made an original comment during the entire interaction.

He did not say, "What do you mean if I am the Son of God? Of course I am." He never drew on His own wit. He never even relied on His own power. He simply responded with the truth of His Father's Word. That was all it took. Nothing creative. Nothing fancy. Just the plain truth directed at the deception behind each of Satan's requests.

The lesson is unmistakably clear. If the only One who ever lived a sinless life combated temptation with God's Word, how do we hope to survive without it? I am so glad He did outsmart Satan in a battle of the minds. I have tried that and failed miserably. I am glad He did not discuss the temptation with Satan and resist him that way. Eve tried that, and she got nowhere. I am glad Jesus did not use raw willpower, though I imagine He could have. My willpower is pretty useless when Satan really turns on the steam. Jesus verbally confronted Satan with the truth; and eventually Satan gave up and left. — Charles F. Stanley, *Winning the War within, electronic ed.* (Nashville, TN: Thomas Nelson, 1997), 132–133.

4. **Review. What is the application of last week's lesson from Matthew 4.3, 4?**

Jesus said, "Man shall not live by bread alone, but by every word that proceeds from the mouth of God" (Matthew 4:4). God's Word provides life and injects it with all that makes you want to live it. Once you begin to direct your life according to the Word of God, life in Christ takes on a full, rich, and exciting meaning. — John MacArthur, *Welcome to the Family:*

What to Expect Now That You're a Christian (Nashville, TN: Nelson Books, 2004), 24–25.

5. **Do temptations come from the inside or the outside? Are the internal or external?**

What is clear from the account is that the temptations came to Jesus from outside of himself, for we are told that the devil "came to" Jesus, "took him" to the holy city, and "took him" to a very high mountain. This is not unimportant, for the only way Jesus could have been tempted was from an outside force and not internally. When we are tempted, we are assailed by an enemy within as well as by temptations from without. In fact, as James says, "Each one is tempted when, by his own evil desire, he is dragged away and enticed" (James 1:14). We are tempted by our fleshly natures, as well as by the world and the devil. Jesus, who had no sinful nature, could only be tempted from something outside himself, which is what happens in this account. — James Montgomery Boice, *The Gospel of Matthew* (Grand Rapids, MI: Baker Books, 2001), 55.

6. **Note that Satan used Scripture in this temptation. What does that tell us? What is the application?**

What a sobering thought that Satan knows Scripture and knows how to use it for his own purposes! Sometimes friends or associates will present attractive and convincing reasons why you should try something that you believe is wrong. They may even find Bible verses that seem to support their viewpoint. Study the Bible carefully, especially the broader contexts of specific verses, so that you understand God's principles for living and what he wants for your life. Only if you really understand what the whole Bible says will you be able to recognize errors of interpretation when people take verses out of context to make them say what they want them to say. Choose your Bible teachers carefully. We have much to learn from others. Capable and wise teachers often present the broader context to help us grow in our Bible knowledge. — Bruce B. Barton, *Matthew, Life Application*

Bible Commentary (Wheaton, IL: Tyndale House Publishers, 1996), 61.

7. **If you have a phone or tablet, do a search for pictures of "highest point temple Jesus temptation." What did you come up with?**

http://holylandtraveljournal.blogspot.com/2012/05/byu-jerusalem-center-caiphas-palace.html

8. **What would you say is at the core of this second temptation?**

"Throw yourself down," Satan says. Then, he insinuates, when Jesus floats down to the ground, he will know that God cares for him. What a thing to have in memory's horde through years of arduous ministry. What a proof of the Father's love! But the valid desire for assurance degenerates into the vice of wanting divine knowledge if Jesus would put God to the test by jumping from the temple.

The temptation is to know in order to be in control. The result of the temptation is that Jesus would live by knowledge, not by faith. Augustine warns against a vain lust to know. There is, he says, an "empty desire to possess" knowledge, a lust to see something new and strange, to satisfy morbid curiosity. To study is a virtue, but vain curiosity is a vice. We do not always need to know and see. Sometimes we should be content to live by faith, not sight.

Students, teachers, professional talkers, leaders, and planners are most susceptible to this temptation. At a minimum, knowledge workers are tempted to pretend we know. At worst, we want the prestige that comes from knowledge. At best, we want to be genuine experts, so we can impart germane information and wisdom both to ordinary folk and to other leaders to guide effective action. Educated people must especially beware the danger of seeking knowledge that is like God's or knowledge that lets us think we do not need God. — Daniel M. Doriani, *Matthew*, ed. Richard D. Phillips, Philip Graham Ryken, and Daniel M. Doriani*, vol. 1, Reformed Expository Commentary* (Phillipsburg, NJ: P&R Publishing, 2008), 74.

9. **Satan has not likely tempted you to jump off any temples. What has he tempted you to do? What is the application for us?**

Satan tempted Christ to advance the work of God by spectacular and obviously worldly means, which is exactly what many evangelicals are doing today when they try to impress people with so-called "signs and wonders" or by entertainment reminiscent of television. We cannot accomplish invisible spiritual work by outward worldly means. At the same time, the devil's suggestion was also a temptation to spiritual presumption, to demand a supernatural sign from God in response to an action he had neither encouraged nor commanded. — James Montgomery Boice, *The Gospel of Matthew* (Grand Rapids, MI: Baker Books, 2001), 56–57.

10. Matthew 4.6. Compare this with Psalm 91. How did Satan misquote this verse?

Quoting Psalm 91, verses 11 and 12, Satan now questions the Father's protection. "Do You believe Your Father will really protect You, Jesus? Prove it. Prove it to Yourself, prove it to me, and prove it to all of Israel. Go to the pinnacle of the temple and jump down. Doesn't Psalm 91 declare that God will give His angels charge over You to keep You from even stubbing Your toe?"

Satan quotes Scripture, but always omits a phrase or two in the process. Psalm 91, verse 11 actually says, "For he shall give his angels charge over thee, to keep thee in all thy ways"—in all God's ways. Jesus knew this and answered accordingly. — Jon Courson, *Jon Courson's Application Commentary* (Nashville, TN: Thomas Nelson, 2003), 22.

11. What is the significance of this change?

Satan was quoting Scripture out of context, making it sound as though God protects even through sin, removing the natural consequences of sinful acts. Neither jumping from the roof in a public display or jumping in order to test God's promises would have been part of God's will for Jesus. In context, the psalm promises God's protection for those who, while being in his will and serving him, find themselves in danger. It does not promise protection for artificially created crises in which Christians call to God in order to test his love and care. We should not test God, as Jesus will explain (see the following verse). — Bruce B. Barton, *Matthew, Life Application Bible Commentary* (Wheaton, IL: Tyndale House Publishers, 1996), 61.

12. How did Jesus respond to this temptation? What is the lesson for us?

Jesus replied to this suggestion by another quotation from Deuteronomy: "It is also written: 'Do not put the Lord your God to the test' " (Matt. 4:7; see Deut. 6:16). He meant, "Satan, you want me to test God, but you have to understand that God is not the one who is to be tested. I am the one being tested, and that means my responsibility is not to challenge my Father but to trust him."

In this reply, Jesus introduced an important principle of sound Bible study, which is not only to trust the Word of God implicitly and absolutely (that is what the first temptation was about) but to interpret Scripture with Scripture, never taking a verse out of context but rather interpreting it by use of other verses or the Bible as a whole. This is what the Protestant reformers called "the analogy of faith," meaning that Scripture interprets itself (Scriptura sui interpres). The Westminster divines expressed it well when they said, "The infallible rule of interpretation of Scripture is the Scripture itself: and therefore, when there is a question about the true and full sense of any Scripture (which is not manifold, but one), it must be searched and known by other places that speak more clearly" (The Westminster Confession of Faith, 1, ix).

This does not mean we will not encounter passages of the Bible that are difficult for us to understand. On the contrary, it suggests we will encounter such passages. But at the same time it says that God is the author of Scripture, and for that reason, the statements of Scripture will always complement and reinforce each other when rightly understood. If they do not do this, God is speaking with a forked tongue, which is impossible for him to do. Jesus knew this, which was why he appealed to Deuteronomy 6:16 to reject the devil's temptation. When taken as a whole, the Bible will always provide for a consistent and God-trusting way of life. — James Montgomery Boice, *The Gospel of Matthew* (Grand Rapids, MI: Baker Books, 2001), 57.

13. Let's look at Psalm 91. What do we learn about God from this Psalm?

All the psalms are from God and are wonderful. But some have commended themselves to God's people as being especially rich and comforting and to which they have repeatedly turned in times of sickness, loneliness, and trouble. Psalm 91 is one of these special psalms. It has been committed to heart by thousands of people, and millions have turned to it with thankfulness in the midst of life's calamities.

Psalm 91 may be compared with Psalm 46, which calls God "our refuge and strength, an ever-present help in trouble" (Ps. 46:1). Martin Luther loved that psalm and turned to it often because he had so many troubles. Psalm 91 may also be compared with Psalm 90. Both call God the "dwelling place" of his people, which is probably why they have been placed together in the Psalter. There are verbal similarities between the two psalms, which has led some commentators to conclude that Psalm 91, as well as Psalm 90, was written by Moses, though there are no other truly substantial reasons for thinking that. Besides, the psalms differ greatly in their tones. As H. C. Leupold says, "The latter [Psalm 90] is somber and stately; this is bright and simple. The one breathes deep insight; the other cheerful trust."

Charles Haddon Spurgeon was not overstating the case when he wrote, "In the whole collection there is not a more cheering psalm; its tone is elevated and sustained throughout, faith is at its best and speaks nobly." — James Montgomery Boice, *Psalms 42–106: An Expositional Commentary* (Grand Rapids, MI: Baker Books, 2005), 747.

14. **A great practice for every Christian is to pray the scriptures. Pray about what you read about. (Do a search on Amazon for books dealing with this; there are lots.) How would you turn this Psalm into a prayer? Let's pause just now and voice a prayer in response to this Psalm?**

Father, I thank You for the vivid picture You paint in Your Word as You promise to cover me with Your feathers and grant me refuge under Your wings; Your faithfulness will be my shield and rampart. I need not fear the terror of night, nor the arrow that flies by day, nor the pestilence that stalks in the darkness, nor the plague that destroys at midday. A thousand may fall at my side, ten thousand at my right hand, but You will keep destruction from coming near me. (Ps. 91:4–7)

Lord God, I love Your Word! You offer to rescue those who love You and protect those who acknowledge Your name. I will call upon You, and You will answer me; You will be with me in trouble, You will deliver me and honor me. Lord, I ask You to satisfy me with long life and show me Your salvation. (Ps. 91:14–16)

—Beth Moore, *Praying God's Word* (Nashville: B&H, 2009).

15. Let's make a list of all of the things we are promised protection from.

These verses spell out the particular dangers which God's promise of protection covers. They read like an insurance policy! It covers snares (v. 3a), pestilence (v. 3b), violent attacks from enemies (vv. 5–8), safety both for your person and your home (vv. 9–10) and angelic protection from the rigours of the journey and from wild beasts (vv. 11–13). We Christians with our relatively settled life in peaceful communities may not find some of these particularly relevant, but our Christian pathway through the world is beset with difficulties: from the people of the world, from false teachers, from the devil and from our own sinful natures. God's protection covers these equally and verse 4 certainly applies directly to us. — Eric Lane, *Psalms 90-150: The Lord Reigns, Focus on the Bible Commentary* (Scotland: Christian Focus Publications, 2006), 14.

16. Does God always protect us from all these things?

Some argue that the teachings of this psalm are simply not true. They think of someone who was not protected from or delivered from calamity and conclude on that basis that this psalm is mistaken. What are we to say about this? The following should be kept in mind:

1. Most of the time God does keep us from calamity. John Calvin says, 'When we look back on our life from the perspective of eternity, we are going to see that the power of Satan was so great, that the weakness of our flesh was feeble, and that the hostility of the world was so strong, that every day of our lives—if God had not intervened—we would never have made it through a day.'

2. Sometimes God allows calamities to come upon us for our good. Matthew Henry says: 'Though trouble or affliction befall thee, yet there shall be no real evil in it, for it shall come from the love of God and shall be sanctified; and it shall come, not for thy hurt, but for thy good; and though, for the present, it be not joyous but grievous, yet, in the end, it shall yield so well that thou thyself shall own no evil befel thee.'

3. When God does allow something hurtful to come into our lives, he is there to strengthen us and to help us bear it. — Roger Ellsworth, *Opening up Psalms, Opening Up Commentary* (Leominster: Day One Publications, 2006), 40–41.

17. Back to Matthew 4.7. What does it mean to put the Lord to a test?

God cannot be manipulated. God is not our magician in the sky ready to perform on request. In response to Satan's temptations, Jesus said not to put God to a test (Deuteronomy 6:16). You may want to ask God to do something to prove his existence or his love for you. A man once asked Jesus that a special sign be sent to help people believe. Jesus told him that people who don't believe what is written in the Bible wouldn't believe even if someone were to come back from the dead to warn them (Luke 16:31)! God wants us to live by faith, not by magic. Don't try to manipulate God by asking for signs. — Neil S. Wilson, *The Handbook of Bible Application* (Carol Stream, IL: Tyndale House Publishers, Inc., 2000), 391.

18. We always want to study the Bible for practical application. What would it look like for one of us to put the Lord to a test?

When I was a pastor, some of the members of my church unwittingly yielded to the temptation to put God to the test. I had a dear friend who was dying of cancer. But word spread around the church that four independent "witnesses" all testified that Dick wasn't going to die because God had told them so. Several exclaimed, "Isn't it wonderful that God is going to heal Dick!" Three weeks later Dick was dead.

If God was the One who told these four people that Dick wasn't going to die, then what does that make God? A liar. But is God a liar? Of course not; He's the truth. The originator of this "good news" was obviously the father of lies. Deceiving spirits had circulated a lie about Dick in an attempt to create a false hope and destroy the congregation's confidence in God.

God is under no obligation to us; He is under obligation only to Himself. There is no way you can cleverly word a prayer so that God must respond to it. That not only distorts the meaning of prayer but puts us in the position of manipulating God. The righteous shall live by faith in the written Word of God and not demand that God prove Himself in response to our whims or wishes, no matter how noble they may be. We are the ones being tested, not God. — Neil Anderson, *The Bondage Breaker: Overcoming *negative Thoughts *irrational Feelings *habitual Sins* (Eugene, OR: Harvest House, 2006).

19. Malachi 3.10 says, "test me in this." What is the difference?

We must distinguish this from the use in Malachi 3:10, where the Lord says to Israel, 'Test me in this (prove me now, AV) and see whether I will not throw open the flood gates of heaven and pour out so much blessing that you will not have room enough for it.' This testing is not a sinful demand for further assurance. It is relying on God to keep the word he has already given, in the appropriate circumstances, not demanding proof beforehand. — John Legg, *The King and His Kingdom: The Gospel of Matthew Simply Explained, Welwyn Commentary Series* (Darlington, England: Evangelical Press., 2004), 50.

20. What do you want to recall from today's discussion?

21. How can we support one another in prayer this week?

Desert Reign

OPEN

What is your name and one thing you are grateful for.

DIG

1. Review. I can resist anything except temptation. Tell me one thing you have learned so far on dealing with temptation.

No safety measures can perfectly "sin-proof" our lives. The Bible makes it clear that we are weak and will not experience ultimate victory over sin in this life. Nevertheless, we are called to wrestle against sin and advised to establish boundaries of protection from its influence. When we fall down, we must pick ourselves up again and continue the race. Here are some suggestions for making the race safer:

1) Admit to yourself that you have a problem. Identifying the problem is half the solution. You may have more successes than failures in the area of lust. More power to you. Whether your struggle is hourly, daily, or weekly, acknowledge that lust is a weakness that would yield fruit if the opportunity presented itself under less-than-ideal circumstances.

2) Admit to someone else that you have a problem. Often Christians who fall prey to sexual sin do not have an accountability partner. Get one. Give someone permission to ask you any question he chooses. Don't lie to this person. Give him permission to take over your computer with no advanced notice and search your Internet history.

3) Remove stumbling blocks from your life. Identify your vulnerabilities. What time of day are you most susceptible to sexual fantasies? Where are you? Are you alone? Eliminate the vehicles in your life that bring temptation into your path. Replace them with prayer and Scripture memory.

4) Flee from sexual immorality. The Bible teaches us to stand firm against the devil, but to flee from sexual immorality. That should convince us of the power this sin wields in our lives. Train yourself to flee from situations that lend themselves to compromise.

5) Confess your sins. Some men have already gone too far. They have made sexual decisions that jeopardize their marriage and their witness for Christ. But too far does not necessarily mean too late. God offers forgiveness when we turn from our sins. Accept responsibility for your actions before God and, if you are married, before your spouse. — Jeffrey E. Miller, Hazards of Being a Man: Overcoming *12 Challenges All Men Face* (Grand Rapids, MI: Baker, 2007).

2. Overview. Who can recall all three temptations of Jesus in the wilderness?

You might show your group this video: https://www.youtube.com/watch?v=ixfYkAHjAgM

3. Can you think of other times in Jesus life when He was tempted?

The "temptation" of Jesus is closely related to His vocation as Messiah. Would He succumb to the false messianic ideals of contemporary Judaism, or choose God's way of the Suffering Servant? The temptations were real, whether external and literal, internal and mental, or a combination of both. He did not pretend to be tempted, but by resisting the temptation to sin, Jesus demonstrated His qualifications to be God's Messiah and humanity's Sin-Bearer. Jesus will meet the temptations summarized here (vv. 1–11; Mark 1:12, 13; Luke 4:1–13) throughout His ministry: when the crowds want only a healer (Mark 1:35–39), when they want to make Him King (John 6:14, 15), when His disciples reject a Suffering Servant Messiah (16:21–28), and finally when He is in Gethsemane (26:36–46). "The devil" is diabolos (Gk.), "slanderer." By use of the definite article, Matthew identifies him as a real person, not just an evil influence (cf. Ezek. 28:12; also see chart, "Names for Satan" in Mark). — W. A. Criswell et al., eds., *Believer's Study Bible, electronic ed*. (Nashville: Thomas Nelson, 1991), Mt 4:1.

4. We talked about the importance of Scripture memory. What kind of progress are you making in this vital discipline?

If we are to live and labor among the lost, that means we need to be doing what we do where the people are. Right now, where people are is on their cell phones. According to *The New York Times*, the International Telecommunication Union predicts the number of mobile subscriptions in the world will pass five billion this year.

The folks at NavPress saw a great opportunity to begin developing discipleship tools that are available to people in a format that they're used to using. Last fall the NavPress team took a classic Navigator tool, The Topical Memory System (TMS), and created an iPhone application that allows people to memorize Scripture and check their progress—on their cell phones.

"We had already developed a desktop version of the TMS," said Michael Visentine, chief operating officer of NavPress. "About 350 people have already downloaded it. We adapted it and created an app for the iPhone, and submitted it to Apple. We expect it to be available by mid-summer."

Although the iPhone application is their first foray into developing tools for mobile devices, the potential impact is significant. "There are many areas in the world," explains Michael, "where people will never use books. Production and distribution is too costly and cumbersome. But even in those areas, cell phone use is growing. This allows us to get helpful tools into the hands of people who might otherwise never have access to them." http://www.navigators.org/Tools/ Newsletters/Featured%20Newsletters/One%20To%20One/June-July%202010/June-July%202010/Scripture%20Memory-%20 There-s%20an%20App%20for%20That

5. **The first temptation was to turn stones into bread. The second was to jump off the temple. What was the third?**

Lust of the eyes: 'The devil took him to a very high mountain and showed him all the kingdoms of the world and their splendour. "All this I will give you" he said, "if you will bow down and worship me" ' (4:8–9). (Matthew gives this as the third temptation but Luke gives it as the second.) Satan's strategy was to appeal to his senses and 'show him all the kingdoms of the world', to try to awaken a covetousness that would steer him from his course. — Charles Price, *Matthew: Can Anything Good Come Out of Nazareth?, Focus on the Bible Commentary* (Fearn, Great Britain: Christian Focus Publications, 1998), 44.

6. **Where did the devil take Jesus?**

The third temptation may occur in a vision (though no less real a test), since there are no places from which one can literally see "all the kingdoms of the world" (v. 8). Worshiping Satan is by far the worst of his three demands since "the Lord your God" alone (v. 10) should be adored (Deut 6:13). Jesus does claim authority over all the cosmos but cannot do so if he bypasses the cross. Scripture has already demonstrated this. He will rescue those who want salvation but not those implacably opposed to him. — D. A. Carson, "The Gospels and Acts," *in NIV Zondervan Study Bible: Built on the Truth of Scripture and Centered on the Gospel Message*, ed. D. A. Carson (Grand Rapids, MI: Zondervan, 2015), 1935.

7. Which of the Ten Commandments is the devil tempting Jesus to break?

The concern of the third temptation is idolatry, as seen in the sequel to Jesus' deuteronomic response. Immediately following the command, "You shall fear the LORD your God; you shall serve him, and swear by his name," we read, "You shall not go after other gods, of the gods of the peoples who are round about you" (Deut. 6:13–14). Despite this and many other warnings, Israel repeatedly "played the harlot" with other gods (Exod. 32:1–6; Judg. 2:17; etc.). Their love for the Lord their God (Deut. 6:4) was "like a morning cloud, like the dew that goes early away" (Hos. 6:4). — Douglas R. A. Hare, *Matthew, Interpretation, a Bible Commentary for Teaching and Preaching* (Louisville, KY: John Knox Press, 1993), 25.

8. Verse 9. Was the world the Devil's to give? Did he have the authority to fulfill this promise?

The devil's dominion over all the world, implied here and explicit in Luke 4:6, is stated also in John 12:31 (cf. 2 Cor. 4:4; 1 John 5:19). It was this dominion which Jesus had come to contest, and the contest would be fierce. To avoid it by compromise with the devil was not a very subtle temptation, but it provided a crucial test of Jesus' loyalty to his Father, even where it meant renouncing the easy way of allowing the end to justify the means. (After all, Jesus' mission was to achieve world-wide dominion: Dan. 7:14; cf. Matt. 28:18.) Israel had fallen to this temptation again and again, and had renounced their exclusive loyalty to God for the sake of political advantage. At the entry to the promised land the temptation met them in an acute form (Deut. 6:10–15; Jesus' reply quotes v. 13). But the true Son of God cannot compromise his loyalty, and sharply dismisses the devil, using now for the first time the name which reveals his true purpose, Satan, 'the enemy' (of God and of his purpose of salvation). — R. T. France, *Matthew: An Introduction and Commentary, vol. 1, Tyndale New Testament Commentaries* (Downers Grove, IL: InterVarsity Press, 1985), 104–105.

9. **We always want to read the Bible for application. What is the application of this temptation to our lives?**

The Word is clear; only God is to be worshiped. When anything (even a worthy goal) takes the place of the worship of God, Satan gains control. The kingdom that Christ sought would be lost. Never does the end justify the means. — Arthur K. Robertson, *Matthew, Everyman's Bible Commentary* (Chicago, IL: Moody Press, 1983), 31.

10. **Notice verse 11. The devil left him. What do we learn about the devil from this?**

Jesus says, "Be gone," and Satan leaves him. Temptations are always temporary. This is a grace of God. If you can "[r]esist the devil … he will flee from you" (see James 4:7). Our God only allows Satan to tempt us for our good, to try and test and refine our faith. And as 1 Corinthians 10:13 makes clear, there is no temptation (1) that is not common to everyone—don't think your particular temptation is so tough that no one else struggles with it, (2) that is not beyond your ability to resist with our Lord's help—Jesus is "able to help those who are being tempted" (Hebrews 2:18), and (3) from which God does not provide a way of escape—if you say, "No," the devil will go.

Temptations are tough, but they are temporary. Remember that. Say to yourself, "If I can just get through this, if I can just say 'be gone' like Jesus did, or run out of the room as Joseph did with Potiphar's wife, then the devil will gain no foothold." But if you give him an inch, stay in the room longer than you should, or toy with the temptation, then watch out. He'll have you by the heel, then the leg, then the heart.

Temptations are tough but always temporary. Resist the devil, and he will flee from you. — Douglas Sean O'Donnell, *Matthew: All Authority in Heaven and on Earth, ed. R. Kent Hughes, Preaching the Word* (Wheaton, IL: Crossway, 2013), 89.

11. James 4.7 is a good cross reference. Does anyone have that classic verse committed to memory?

When the Bible tells us to "submit to God," and to "resist the devil" (James 4:7), it doesn't mean we're to go out and attack the devil. The devil will do the attacking. The word "resist" is essentially a defensive word meaning "to withstand an attack."

Nor does the Bible say to "converse with the devil and he will flee from us" or to "consider all of the temptations the devil offers, then resist him, and he will flee from us." Once you start messing with sin and with the devil, it's only a matter of time before you get hooked. It's like the free samples you're offered when you walk though the store or the mall. You're given just enough to whet your appetite, but not enough to satisfy it.

The devil has been at this for a long time. He's no idiot, and when he tries to tempt you away from God's path, he won't present his full agenda. Instead, he will say, "Take just a little nibble. Just have a taste for the fun of it. It won't hurt you. Just this one little time." And you know the rest of that story. This is why the Bible tells us to resist the devil. Keep as much distance from him as possible. Flee from temptation—and don't leave a forwarding address.

So where do we find the resolve and strength to resist? We need to submit to God as we resist the devil. "Submit" is a word used to describe a soldier under the authority of a commander and speaks of a willing, conscious submission to God's authority. It means to completely surrender yourself to the Word and will of God. That is your best defense.

And after you have successfully resisted the evil one, don't relax your guard. It's true that the devil may flee when resisted, but he'll be back! Satan and his demons will simply regroup and attack you from yet another angle. The lesson? For the rest of our lives, we must stay alert and vigilant, fully submitted to the will of God. — Greg Laurie, *Daily Hope for Hurting Hearts: A Devotional* (Dana Point, CA: Kerygma Publishing—Allen David Books, 2011).

12. How exactly do we resist the devil? Be very, very practical.

The Bible tells us to stand firm and hold out. James 4:7 promises us that if we resist the devil, he will flee. There is a variety of ways to see that delightful sight of the enemy hightailing it away.

First, we can take into our hands the sword of the Spirit, which is the Word of God. That's what Jesus did, if you remember His wilderness temptation with the devil. As I study that passage, I smile because Jesus fired Scripture at the devil—but He only used ammunition from Deuteronomy. He defended Himself with only one book!

The result of it, as the Scriptures tell us, is that Satan departed from Him. That's another word for fled. Resist the devil and you'll be treated to the sight of his back as he runs away. Recognize, request help, resist. — David Jeremiah, *Slaying the Giants in Your Life* (Nashville, TN: W Pub., 2001), 97–98.

13. This verse says to resist the devil. Are there verses that tell us to flee?

Wise believers recognize that there are degrees of difference in the perils we face. Good military leaders recognize this same principle: There is a time to resist and a time to retreat. Sometimes we need to see the devil flee; sometimes we need to do the fleeing. "There are several good protections against temptations," Mark Twain said, "but the surest is cowardice." There are times when cowardice is another word for wisdom. The Bible gives us three kinds of sins to flee.

1. Flee from idolatry. "Therefore my beloved, flee from idolatry" (1 Corinthians 10:14). This is from the very passage we're studying in this chapter.

An idol is anything that comes between you and God. Anything of value to you could be an idol. When you begin to realize that something is taking the place of God in your life, you don't need to sit and ponder it. You don't need to write a thesis or call a meeting about it. You need to flee! Every moment of personal idolatry is a moment of spiritual danger. It is wear and tear on your soul. Flee from idolatry.

2. Flee from immorality. Twice in the New Testament we are told to turn tail and run when confronted with immorality:

> Flee sexual immorality. (1 Corinthians 6:18)

> Flee... youthful lusts. (2 Timothy 2:22)

Sexual temptation is a demonic trump card; there's something unique and terrible about its power. The devil uses it for those in ministry, those in marriage, those maturing. He uses it particularly for those perched in precarious positions—those in transition, whether through the storms of adolescence, the trials of marriage, or the temptations of business travel.

The story that immediately comes to mind, of course, is that of Joseph in Genesis 39. He was in a crucial transition between slavery and the respect that could be available through a better position in life. But he caught the eye of his master's wife, and she dismissed all the other servants one day in order to set her web of seduction. When she approached Joseph with her offer, he did just what the Bible prescribes—he fled. He turned to run so quickly that the woman was left holding his coat in her hand. It's a good thing that God made young feet swift; they need to be ready to flee from temptations to dishonor God through sexual immorality.

3. Flee from greed. Only in recent years have I discovered this third "flight advisory." I knew that we should flee from idolatry and immorality, but I hadn't noticed that the Bible also commands us to run from greed:

> For the love of money is a root of all kinds of evil, for which some have strayed from the faith in their greediness, and pierced themselves through with many sorrows. But you, O man of God, flee these things. (1 Timothy 6:10–11)

This is really another form of idolatry, isn't it? But I know you'll agree that it's a form that deserves its own special category, because it's so pervasive in our society. I wonder how many people reading this book see materialism as an issue in their lives. The Bible spares no words about the seriousness of that—"a root of all kinds of evil."

This is so pervasive in our society. All kinds of evils proceed from the mouth of materialism. Don't let greed get its hooks into your life or the lives of your children.

Now let's move on to our fifth checklist item for taming temptation. — David Jeremiah, *Slaying the Giants in Your Life* (Nashville, TN: W Pub., 2001), 98–99.

14. Is temptation a sin? Is it a sin to be tempted? Do we have a moral obligation to avoid temptation if we can?

There is a story about a man who was overweight. He became very serious about maintaining a diet, and he worked out every detail, planning his life accordingly. He even changed his route for driving to work because he didn't want to drive by the bakery.

For about a week, he did marvelously. Isn't that always the way with diets? All his coworkers were proud of him. One morning, as they stood around the coffeepot talking about his progress, he came in carrying a dozen doughnuts and a cheesecake. Everyone was aghast. They asked him what happened, and he told them, "I forgot and drove my old route to work today." He smiled. "And I decided that if God wanted me to stop at the bakery, He'd give me a parking space right in front of the main entrance. And you know, He did just that on the eighth trip around the block!"

It's easy to find ways to force our faith into the cookie cutter of our desires, isn't it? But the Bible tells us to take a different road entirely. The doughnut lover should read Proverbs 4:14–15: "Do not enter the path of the wicked, and do not walk in the way of evil. Avoid it, do not travel on it; turn away from it and pass on."

A man told the doctor his arm was broken in two places, and the doctor said, "Well, stop going to those two places." Good advice, but Paul put it even better: "Make no provision for the flesh" (Romans 13:14).

Go home by another way. — David Jeremiah, *Slaying the Giants in Your Life* (Nashville, TN: W Pub., 2001), 99–100.

15. What good things come our way when we avoid temptation when it is in our power to do so?

I
I walk down the street.
There is a deep hole in the sidewalk
I fall in.
I am lost…
I am hopeless.
It isn't my fault.
It takes forever to find a way out.

II
I walk down the same street.
There is a deep hole in the sidewalk.
I pretend I don't see it.
I fall in again.
I can't believe I'm in the same place.

But it isn't my fault.
It still takes a long time to get out.

III
I walk down the same street.
There is a deep hole in the sidewalk.
I see it is there.
I still fall in...it's a habit
My eyes are open; I know where I am;
It is my fault.
I get out immediately.

IV
I walk down the same street.
There is a deep hole in the sidewalk.
I walk around it.

V
I walk down another street.

http://www.ram.org/contrib/autobiography_in_five_chapters.
html

16. How worried are you about dealing with temptation? Is it a big deal?

Forewarned is forearmed. Never fall into the trap of false
security. If I've heard this once, I've heard it a thousand times:
"I can't believe it happened to me!"

Oh, really? Why not you? If the Son of God could experience
every single temptation known to man, that should be a clue
that you're not bigger than the system. People believe that
their commitment to Christ, their spirituality, their knowledge
of the Bible, or their church attendance will place them
beyond temptation. It simply isn't true. In battle, the enemy's
best weapon is surprise. Don't let the devil sneak up on you.

Remember the first words of our passage? "Therefore let him
who thinks he stands take heed lest he fall" (1 Corinthians
10:12). In other words, as soon as you flex your muscles and

begin to admire yourself in the mirror, that's the best moment for someone to pull the rug out from under you! Remember the advance billing of the Titanic? "Even God couldn't sink it." The truth is that if you drift into arrogance, not even God can get through to you. So avoid those delusions of spiritual grandeur.

Dr. Howard Hendricks was my professor at Dallas Seminary, and he remains a close friend today. He used to carry a little notebook around in his pocket. It listed the names of ministers and students from his classes who had fallen into sexual temptation and out of the ministry. At one time, he said, there were more than a hundred names on that list. One day as he was looking through the list, he began to wonder what all those poor souls on the casualty list had in common. These were names he knew—friends, students. He pored over them again and concluded that all, with the exception of two, shared in common a spirit of pride and arrogance.

Proverbs 16:18 tells us that pride precedes destruction, and a haughty spirit leads to a fall. — David Jeremiah, *Slaying the Giants in Your Life* (Nashville, TN: W Pub., 2001), 96–97.

17. Matthew 26:41 What does it mean, "Watch and pray"?

Twice in the New Testament, Jesus tells us to pray about temptation. We're well-advised to take those two admonitions seriously. First we have the Lord's Prayer, which includes, "And do not lead us into temptation, but deliver us from the evil one" (Matthew 6:13). Second we have Matthew 26:41, in which Jesus said to "watch and pray, lest you enter into temptation."

Watch and pray. The idea is to be alert. We need to begin every day asking God to sharpen our antennae toward the devil's ploys. We want God to help us see through the devil's bait-and-switch tactics, and to discern the spiritual reality and its consequences. We should also ask God to make us sensitive to that moment of awareness, the escape hatch that offers safety.

Otherwise, temptation springs upon us without warning. It will catch us at our very worst. If we knew that heavy anvils were falling out of buildings today, we'd walk down the city street with our neck craned, watching the windows. Every day carries hazards for the Christian. We need to pray constantly for awareness and strength. — David Jeremiah, *Slaying the Giants in Your Life* (Nashville, TN: W Pub., 2001), 97.

18. Summary. What do we learn about dealing with temptation from Jesus' example in Matthew 4?

Jesus' experience provides us with mighty wisdom. The most important factor in fighting temptation is to be filled with the Spirit of Christ, the Holy Spirit (Romans 8:9). Christ is the victor over temptation and sin. His very words to us are, "[T] ake heart! I have overcome the world" (John 16:33).

When Martin Luther was asked how he overcame the Devil, he replied, "Well, when he comes knocking upon the door of my heart, and asks 'Who lives here?' the dear Lord Jesus goes to the door and says, 'Martin Luther used to live here, but he has moved out. Now I live here.'" When Christ fills our lives, Satan has no entrance. — R. Kent Hughes, *Mark: Jesus, Servant and Savior, vol. 1, Preaching the Word* (Westchester, IL: Crossway Books, 1989), 32.

19. Is it possible to beat temptation in any way other than the way Jesus did it—by memorizing and using the Word in temptation? Is there an easier way?

The other factor in fighting temptation is to be filled with God's Word. In response to each of the three temptations, Christ answered with Scripture (Deuteronomy 8:3, 6:16, and 6:13). He knew the truth of, "I have hidden your word in my heart that I might not sin against you" (Psalm 119:11). Why is this so? God's Word reveals God's mind, and God's mind cannot be subject to sin. Therefore, if we fill our hearts with his Word, sin and temptation cannot dominate. — R. Kent Hughes, *Mark: Jesus, Servant and Savior, vol. 1, Preaching the Word* (Westchester, IL: Crossway Books, 1989), 32.

20. How can we support one another in prayer this week?

Tempted and Tried Lesson #5
Where the Wild Things Aren't
Good Questions Have Groups Talking
www.joshhunt.com

If you have some readers in your group, you might ask them to read Joyce Meyer's book *Battlefield of the Mind* and give your group a little overview.

Where the Wild Things Aren't

OPEN
What is your name and who was your high school football team's #1 enemey?

DIG
1. **Throughout this study, we have talked about dealing with temptation the way Jesus did—through memorized Scripture. Why is scripture memory valuable to the believer?**

    When you get involved in building up an arsenal of verses, you will be in the process of doing something else as well— renewing your mind. To renew something is a two-stage process. It involves removing the old and putting on the new. When you fill your mind with the truth of God's Word so that you can root out the error that keeps you from being victorious, you are renewing your mind.

The importance of this process cannot be overemphasized. It guards you against falling prey to temptation and it protects you from being brainwashed by the world. This is what Paul was talking about when he wrote,

> And do not be conformed to this world, but be transformed by the renewing of your mind, that you may prove what the will of God is, that which is good and acceptable and perfect. —Romans 12:2

The "how to" of defending ourselves against becoming like the world is to renew our minds. Everywhere we turn we find ourselves being asked to adopt a way of thinking that is contrary to what Christ and His church stand for. Unless you and I make some effort to combat this onslaught of propaganda, we will fall victim to its debilitating poison. — Charles F. Stanley, *Winning the War Within*, electronic ed. (Nashville, TN: Thomas Nelson, 1997), 142–143.

2. **Overview. 2 Corinthians 2.11. Paul says we are not to be unaware of the devil's schemes. What does the Bible teach about the devil?**

Satan is a powerful spirit being...not a myth, not a cartoon character in a red suit with a pitchfork, and not "the dark side of the force," lacking identity or personality. He is real, and Scripture calls him by name.

We're talking about an active personality with an agenda here, not an impersonal force. Satan has something he very much wants to accomplish.

And what is that? The devil's single, consuming ambition is to turn you and me away from God and all that is good. His ultimate agenda can be summed up in the statement of Christ in John 10:10, where Jesus said, "The thief's purpose is to steal and kill and destroy. My purpose is to give them a rich and satisfying life" (NLT).

You can immediately see the contrast. Jesus is in effect saying, "I have come to give you life. Satan has come to give you death. I have come to give you freedom. He has come to give you bondage. I have come to build you up, to save you, to restore you. He has come to steal, kill, and destroy." And that is what he wants to do with you to this very day, this very hour.

The devil is very effective at what he does. Never doubt that. Never underestimate his capacity to package his wares, making bad things look good, and good things look bad. He is a master deceiver, and we should never dismiss him or treat him lightly.

Even though we shouldn't become overly preoccupied with our adversary and his activities, it's wise for us to understand his methods of operation. Paul wrote to the Corinthians that they should take a certain course of action "in order that Satan might not outwit us. For we are not unaware of his schemes" (2 Corinthians 2:11, NIV).

Being aware of his schemes and how he operates can help us to effectively resist him. And that is exactly what Scripture tells us to do: "Resist the devil and he will flee from you" (James 4:7, NIV). — Greg Laurie, *Daily Hope for Hurting Hearts: A Devotional* (Dana Point, CA: Kerygma Publishing— Allen David Books, 2011).

3. What bad things happen if we are unaware of his schemes?

The British scholar and writer C. S. Lewis wrote that we generally make one of two errors when considering the devil. Either we give him more attention than he deserves, or we ignore him completely. So where do we find the balance— the truth about the devil?

Not in popular culture. If we think of him with his proverbial red suit, pointy tail, and pitchfork, we make a laughing matter out of something serious. We need an authoritative source for learning about the devil, and that would be the Bible—the only book that chronicles his past, present, and future.

Prayerfully open your Bible for a look at the devil and let God show you how to be wary of his schemes—as well as how God has overwhelmingly defeated him. — David Jeremiah, *1 Minute a Day* (Nashville: Thomas Nelson, 2009).

4. **Ephesians 6.10 – 12. What does this passage teach us about our enemy, the devil? There could be several right answers.**

There is a world about which many of us are unconscious, or unaware. It is real nonetheless. In fact, it is more real than the world we can see, touch, taste, hear, or feel. It is the realm of the spirit.

The most real part of you is your spirit. You are a spirit. Many men seem to think the real part of them is their body, but no matter how much you build it up, manicure it, dress it, or feed it, you are not first and foremost a body. You have a body. You live in a body. It is a temporary home.

You also have a soul. The soulish area of man is where most of the problems occur; this is the area of the mind, the emotions, memories, appetites, desires. The mind of man, including the mind of the Christian, is often trapped between the physical and the spiritual—flashbacks to memories of the former life in the flesh can fill the mind. The result can be a tremendous wrestling match, with each force, spirit and flesh, trying to dominate the other. In fact, it is only when a man receives the Word of God and engrafts it to his mind that he is able to save his mind from the clutches of the flesh.

Demons are disembodied spirits. They don't have a body, and they don't have a soul—they have no mind of their own or will of their own. Their will is totally subjected to Satan. They are vessels and carriers of Satan's nature. They are filled with his desires, his lusts, his passions, and his unclean thoughts.

Because demons don't have bodies, they are seeking one. They are seeking a vehicle through which they can express their lusts and passions for evil.

Jesus once said to Simon Peter, "Simon, Simon, behold, Satan hath desired to have you, that he may sift you as wheat" (Luke 22:31). He was saying to Peter, "Satan desires to possess you, to have you, to dominate you." Men know what it means to lust after a woman in order to have her. That's the way Satan looked at Peter. He lusted after him, that he might completely take Peter's mind and body—to satisfy his cravings through him.

Satan's demons desire the same thing today regarding you—

To use your body, your temper, your lust, your passions.

To work through the broken places of your childhood to fulfill their ravenous desires.

To possess you so that he might sift you. — T. D. Jakes, *So You Call Yourself a Man? A Devotional for Ordinary Men with Extraordinary Potential* (Grand Rapids, MI: Baker, 2007).

5. Should we be worried about what the devil can do to us?

When the enemy knocks at the door or when he prowls around back or when he looks for the chink in your armor, you hang on to Christ. You stand firm in faith. You put on the "armor of God" (Ephesians 6:11–20—please read it!). You have nothing to worry about. Nothing. For, as Peter reminds us, our Lord has "dominion forever and ever." He is the one ultimately in control, and that is something in which every believer can find strength to hope again. — Charles R. Swindoll, *Bedside Blessings: 365 Days of Inspirational Thoughts* (Nashville: Thomas Nelson, 2011).

6. What exactly does it mean to "take your stand"? Be very practical.

Vance Havner used to remark that too many are running for something when they ought to be standing for something. God's people should be willing to stand! We have become so brainwashed in so many ways that Christians are afraid to speak out against uncleanness in any form. The enemy of our souls has persuaded us that Christianity should be a rather casual thing—certainly not something to get excited about.

Fellow Christian, we only have a little time. We are not going to be here very long. Our triune God demands that we engage in those things that will remain when the world is on fire, for fire determines the value and quality of every person's work. — A. W. Tozer and Ron Eggert, *The Tozer Topical Reader, vol. 2* (Camp Hill, PA: WingSpread, 1998), 221.

7. Mark 14.38 says "Watch and pray so that you will not fall into temptation." Is that the same or something different than standing firm?

"Watch." They don't come any more practical than that. Watch. Stay alert. Keep your eyes open. When you see sin coming, duck. When you anticipate an awkward encounter, turn around. When you sense temptation, go the other way.

All Jesus is saying is, "Pay attention." You know your weaknesses. You also know the situations in which your weaknesses are most vulnerable. Stay out of those situations. Back seats. Late hours. Night clubs. Poker games. Bridge parties. Movie theaters. Whatever it is that gives Satan a foothold in your life, stay away from it. Watch out! — Max Lucado, *God⬛s Promises® for You: Scripture Selections from Max Lucado* (Nashvllle: Thomas Nelson, 2007).

8. 2 Corinthians 10.3 – 5. Read for application. What do we learn about Christian living from these verses?

Did you catch the reality of divine power in verse 4? Servants with renewed minds have a perspective on life and a power to live life that is altogether unique—divinely empowered.

That explains how wrongs can be forgiven, and how offenses can be forgotten, and how objectives can be pursued day in and day out without our quitting. It's divine power. God promises that He will pour His power into us (Phil. 4:13) and supply all we need if we will simply operate under His full control. When we think correctly we instantly begin to respond correctly.

How can we "demolish" those things that once blew us away? With Christ living out His very life through ours, that's how. By His power we can give ourselves away again and again and again. And we won't fear the outcome. We won't even feel slighted when we don't get the same treatment in return. Servants, remember, don't "keep score." Dale Galloway tells a story in Dream a New Dream that beautifully illustrates this point.

Little Chad was a shy, quiet young fellow. One day he came home and told his mother, he'd like to make a valentine for everyone in his class. Her heart sank. She thought, "I wish he wouldn't do that!" because she had watched the children when they walked home from school. Her Chad was always behind them. They laughed and hung on to each other and talked to each other. But Chad was never included. Nevertheless, she decided she would go along with her son. So she purchased the paper and glue and crayons. For three whole weeks, night after night, Chad painstakingly made thirty-five valentines.

Valentine's Day dawned, and Chad was beside himself with excitement! He carefully stacked them up, put them in a bag, and bolted out the door. His mom decided to bake him his favorite cookies and serve them up warm and nice with a cool glass of milk when he came home from school. She just knew he would be disappointed . . . maybe that would ease the pain a little. It hurt her to think that he wouldn't get many valentines—maybe none at all.

That afternoon she had the cookies and milk on the table. When she heard the children outside she looked out the window. Sure enough here they came, laughing and having the best time. And, as always, there was Chad in the rear. He walked a little faster than usual. She fully expected him to burst into tears as soon as he got inside. His arms were empty, she noticed, and when the door opened she choked back the tears.

"Mommy has some warm cookies and milk for you."

But he hardly heard her words. He just marched right on by, his face aglow, and all he could say was:

"Not a one . . . not a one."

Her heart sank.

And then he added, "I didn't forget a one, not a single one!" So it is when God is in control of the servant's mind. — Charles R. Swindoll, *Improving Your Serve* (Nashville: Thomas Nelson, 2002).

9. How do we take every thought captive?

It is by this continual "watching over" your thoughts that you begin to take every thought captive unto the obedience of Jesus Christ. (2 Cor. 10:5 KJV.) The Holy Spirit is quick to remind you if your mind is beginning to take you in a wrong direction, then the decision becomes yours. Will you flow in the mind of the flesh or in the mind of the Spirit? One leads to death, the other to life. The choice is yours. Choose life! — *Battlefield of the Mind: Winning the Battle in Your Mind* by Joyce Meyer

10. What is a stronghold? Can you think of an example?

A stronghold is an area in which we are held in bondage (in prison) due to a certain way of thinking. — *Battlefield of the Mind: Winning the Battle in Your Mind* by Joyce Meyer

11. What exactly are the weapons of our warfare?

These "weapons" are the Word received through preaching, teaching, books, tapes, seminars and private Bible study. But we must "abide" (continue) in the Word until it becomes revelation given by inspiration of the Holy Spirit. Continuing is important. In Mark 4:24 Jesus says, ...The measure [of thought and study] you give [to the truth you hear] will be the measure [of virtue and knowledge] that comes back to you....

I repeat, we must continue using the weapon of the Word. Two other spiritual weapons available to us are praise and prayer. Praise defeats the devil quicker than any other battle plan, but it must be genuine heart praise, not just lip service or a method being tried to see if it works. Also, praise and prayer both involve the Word. We praise God according to His Word and His goodness.

Two other spiritual weapons available to us are praise and prayer. Praise defeats the devil quicker than any other battle plan, but it must be genuine heart praise, not just lip service or a method being tried to see if it works. Also, praise and prayer both involve the Word. We praise God according to His Word and His goodness. — *Battlefield of the Mind: Winning the Battle in Your Mind* by Joyce Meyer

12. This all sound very theoretical. What difference does it make to our Monday morning?

Mary and her husband, John, are not enjoying a happy marriage. There is strife between them all the time. They are both angry, bitter and resentful. They have two children who are being affected by the problems in the home. The strife is showing up in their school work and behavior. One of the children is having stomach problems caused by nerves. Mary's problem is that she doesn't know how to let John be the head of their home. She is bossy — she wants to make all the decisions, handle the finances and discipline the children. She wants to work so she will have her "own" money. She is independent, loud, demanding and a nag.

About now you may be thinking, "I've got her answer. She needs to know Jesus." She does know Him! Mary received Jesus as her Savior five years ago — three years after she and John were married. "Do you mean there hasn't been a change in Mary since receiving Jesus as Savior?" Yes, there has been change. She believes she is going to heaven even though her bad behavior causes her to feel constant condemnation. She has hope now. Before she met Jesus, she was miserable and hopeless; now she is just miserable.

Mary knows that her attitude is wrong. She wants to change. She has received counseling from two people, and she gets in almost every prayer line asking for victory over anger, rebellion, unforgiveness, resentment and bitterness. Why hasn't she seen more improvement?

The answer is found in Romans 12:2: Do not be conformed to this world (this age), [fashioned after and adapted to its external, superficial customs], but be transformed (changed) by the [entire] renewal of your mind [by its new ideals and its new attitude], so that you may prove [for yourselves] what is the good and acceptable and perfect will of God, even the thing which is good and acceptable and perfect [in His sight for you]. Mary has strongholds in her mind. They have been there for years. She doesn't even understand how they got there. She knows she shouldn't be rebellious, bossy, nagging, etc., but she doesn't know what to do to change her nature. It seems that she simply reacts in certain situations in an unseemly way because she can't control her actions.

Mary can't control her actions because she doesn't control her thoughts. She doesn't control her thoughts because there are strongholds in her mind that the devil set up early in her life. Satan begins to initiate his well-laid plans and to sow his deliberate deception at a very young age. In Mary's case, her problems started long ago, in childhood. As a child Mary had an extremely domineering father who often spanked her just because he was in a bad mood. If she made one wrong move, he would vent his anger on her. For years, she suffered helplessly as her father mistreated her and her mother. He was disrespectful in all his ways toward his wife and daughter.

Mary's brother, however, could do no wrong. It seemed as if he was favored just because he was a boy. By the time she was sixteen, Mary had been brainwashed for years by Satan who had told her lies that went something like this: "Men really think they are something. They are all alike; you can't trust them. They will hurt you and take advantage of you. If you're a man, you've got it made in life. You can do anything you want. You can order people around, be the boss, treat people any way you please and nobody (especially not wives or daughters) can do anything about it."

As a result, Mary's mind was resolved: "When I get away from here, nobody is ever going to push me around again!" Satan was already waging war on the battlefield of her mind. Play those thoughts over and over in your head a hundred thousand times or more over a period of ten years, and see if you're ready to get married and become a sweet, submissive, adoring wife. Even if by some miracle you should want to be, you won't know how. This is the kind of mess in which Mary finds herself today. What can she do? What can any of us do in such a situation?

Here Jesus tells us how we are to win the victory over the lies of Satan. We must get the knowledge of God's truth in us, renew our minds with His Word, then use the weapons of 2 Corinthians 10:4,5 to tear down strongholds and every high and lofty thing that exalts itself against the knowledge of God. — *Battlefield of the Mind: Winning the Battle in Your Mind* by Joyce Meyer

13. Is it easy or hard to take every thought captive?

When the battle seems endless and you think you'll never make it, remember that you are reprogramming a very carnal, fleshly, worldly mind to think as God thinks. Impossible? No! Difficult? Yes! But, just think, you have God on your team. I believe He is the best "computer programmer" around. (Your mind is like a computer that has had a lifetime of garbage programmed into it.) God is working even on you; at least, He is if you have invited Him to have control of your thoughts. He is reprogramming your mind. Just keep cooperating with Him — and don't give up! It will definitely take time, and it won't all be easy, but you are going in the right direction if you choose God's way of thinking. You will spend your time doing something, so it may as well be going forward and not staying in the same mess for the rest of your life. — *Battlefield of the Mind: Winning the Battle in Your Mind* by Joyce Meyer

14. What are the odds we will win this war? Can we expect to win, or will we just keep fighting and losing the same old battles year after year, decade after decade?

I saw a literal picture of this in a prairie ditch. A petroleum company was hiring strong backs and weak minds to lay a pipeline. Since I qualified, much of a high-school summer was spent shoveling in a shoulder-high, multimile West Texas trough. A large digging machine trenched ahead of us. We followed, scooping out the excess dirt and rocks.

One afternoon the machine dislodged more than dirt. "Snake!" shouted the foreman. We popped out of that hole faster than a jack-in-the-box and looked down at the rattlesnake nest. Big momma hissed, and her little kids squirmed. Reentering the trench was not an option. One worker launched his shovel and beheaded the rattler. We stood on the higher ground and watched as she—now headless—writhed and twisted in the soft dirt below. Though defanged, the snake still spooked us.

Gee, Max, thanks for the inspirational image.

Inspirational? Maybe not. But hopeful? I think so. That scene in the West Texas summer is a parable of where we are in life. Is the devil not a snake? John calls him "that old snake who is the devil" (Rev. 20:2 NCV.).

Has he not been decapitated? Not with a shovel, but with a cross. "God disarmed the evil rulers and authorities. He shamed them publicly by his victory over them on the cross of Christ" (Col. 2:15 NLT.).

So how does that leave us? Confident. The punch line of the passage is Jesus' power over Satan. One word from Christ, and the demons are swimming with the swine, and the wild man is "clothed and in his right mind" (Mark 5:15). Just one command! No séance needed. No hocus-pocus. No chants were heard or candles lit. Hell is an anthill against heaven's steamroller. Jesus "commands … evil spirits, and they obey him" (Mark 1:27 NCV.). The snake in the ditch and Lucifer in the pit—both have met their match. — Max Lucado, *Next Door Savior* (Nashville, TN: W Pub. Group, 2003), 60.

15. Imagine two Christians. One is taking every thought captive. The other is not. How are their lives different? How will their lives be different ten years from now?

Satan knows well that if he can control our thoughts, he can control our actions.

You cannot have a positive life and a negative mind.

Thoughts bear fruit. Think good thoughts, and the fruit in your life will be good. Think bad thoughts, and the fruit in your life will be bad.

A sweet, kind person does not have mean, vindictive thoughts. By the same token, a truly evil person does not have good, loving thoughts. — *Battlefield of the Mind: Winning the Battle in Your Mind* by Joyce Meyer

16. 1 Peter 5.8, 9. What do we learn about Christian living from these verses? There can be multiple right answers.

The devil is already at work. He is painting a target on your back, on your front, or anywhere else you have a weak spot. I could name a few. He is already making plans to do everything he can with his demon accomplices to devastate, denigrate, and destroy your ministry if he can. — James Draper, *Preaching with Passion: Sermons from the Heart of the Southern Baptist Convention* (Nashville: B&H, 2004).

17. What do we learn about the devil? Again, there can be several answers.

There are times when God will allow you to see difficulty as it approaches. When this happens, you can prepare for the battle through prayer and the study of His Word. Other times trouble strikes without warning. His Word offers insight into how He wants us to handle the battle.

Many of the problems we face are direct assaults sent by Satan with one thought in mind: destroy, discourage, disable God's child. Throughout God's Word, we are cautioned to be on the alert against the schemes of the devil (1 Peter 5:8–9).

Peter knew what he was talking about when he cautioned the early church. He understood what it was like to be the target of the enemy's deception, and he was passing on the wisdom he had learned to others.

Every believer will face the same battle at one time or another. While Paul's thorn in the flesh (2 Cor. 12:7) was believed to be physical in nature, it also was a direct result of the enemy's attack. Satan sought to buffet him to the point of spiritual retreat.

Make no mistake about it: If Satan sought to undo Paul with discouragement, he will do the same to us. That is why Paul told us to put on the whole armor of God (Eph. 6:10–18). Claim what God has provided you. This is your greatest shield and protection: His Word and the fact that you belong to Him. — Charles F. Stanley, *Seeking His Face* (Nashville, TN: Thomas Nelson Publishers, 2002), 229.

18. Be practical. How do we resist the devil? I am now going to resist the devil. What do I do?

One last suggestion is to get in the habit of quoting these verses audibly when you are tempted. This may seem a little strange at first, but there are good reasons to do this. First, I do not believe Satan and his host can read our minds. He can put thoughts there, but the Scripture does not indicate that he can read them.

If that is true, simply thinking through a verse poses the enemy no threat. It may help you refocus your attention and therefore relieve the pressure for a time. But in terms of really challenging the devil and putting him in his place, I am not convinced that mentally reviewing Scripture does much good.

The second reason speaking the truth aloud is important is that it shifts the point of tension from an internal conflict to an external one. Throughout this book, I have referred to our tendency to emotionally latch on to temptation and own it as part of our being, to mistakenly think, This is the way I am. Otherwise why would I feel this way?

When you speak the truth out loud, you are reminded that you are not your enemy. And He that is within you is not your enemy. Your enemy is the devil. He roams around like a lion looking for someone to devour (1 Pet. 5:8). Satan hates to be recognized. He would much rather have you internalize the battle so that he can remain anonymous.

There are times when we are our own worst enemy. This is certainly the case when we ignore the principle outlined in chapter 8 and make unwise decisions. But even in those cases, I have found it extremely helpful to speak the truth aloud.

Now I'm not talking about shouting it at the top of your lungs. There are times when you will simply have to whisper it. At other times you can speak in a normal tone of voice. You may feel silly the first time you do this, but you will notice an immediate difference when you do.

When you speak the truth out loud, it is as if you have taken a stand with God against the enemy. When I begin speaking the truth aloud, I often feel a sense of courage and conviction sweeping over me. Usually this turns into joy, and what started out as a bad thing becomes a time of praise and rejoicing. If you don't believe me, just try it.

The last reason I think it is a good idea to speak aloud when tempted is that Jesus did it. Need I say more? — Charles F. Stanley, *Winning the War Within*, electronic ed. (Nashville, TN: Thomas Nelson, 1997), 141–142.

19. **A basic discipline of the Christian life is to wed Bible reading, Bible study, Bible memorization, and Bible mediation with prayer. How could you respond in prayer to this passage?**

Dear heavenly Father, thank You for Your grace and power, which prepare me for battle. — Charles F. Stanley, *Seeking His Face* (Nashville, TN: Thomas Nelson Publishers, 2002), 229.

Father God, help me to be self-controlled and alert. My enemy the devil prowls around like a roaring lion looking for someone to devour. Help me to resist him, standing firm in the faith. I can be assured that other believers throughout the world are undergoing the same kind of sufferings. (1 Pet. 5:8–9) — Beth Moore, *Praying God's Word* (Nashville: B&H, 2009).

20. **What is your take away from today's lesson?**

Made in the USA
Middletown, DE
25 January 2017